For Instance...

By the same author:

THE GIST OF THE LESSON
THE TREASURY OF RELIGIOUS VERSE
THE DICTIONARY OF RELIGIOUS TERMS
FAVORITE CHRISTIAN POEMS
WITH LOVE TO MOTHER
A TREASURY OF GREAT PRAYERS
AMERICA IN VERSE
FOR INSTANCE . . .

1995

For Instance...

CURRENT INSIGHTS, ANECDOTES, QUOTATIONS, QUESTIONS FOR TEACHERS, MINISTERS, SPEAKERS AND DISCUSSION LEADERS

Donald T. Kauffman

1970
DOUBLEDAY & COMPANY, INC., GARDEN CITY, NEW YORK

HOW TO USE THIS BOOK

This book is based on the assumption that no matter what a teacher or speaker is trying to communicate, one illustration is worth a thousand abstractions. Perhaps more in our global village of the 1970s than ever before, the live image and the breathing example blow the mind. An actual "for instance" can often perform the inexplicable miracle of moving an idea from one brain to another.

When Jesus talked about love, he gave that unforgettable example from the happenings of his times about a man mugged in a crime-ridden neighborhood and another man whose honest neighborliness resulted in welding together forever the words "Good" and "Samaritan." I have an idea that today He would use the same kinds of illustrations to make his points, only they would be drawn from the events and circumstances of these fast-changing times.

At a weekend retreat in Reading, Pennsylvania, I read J. Elliott Corbett's modern paraphrase from Jeremiah:

O you Christians, strength of my arm, voice of my mouth, compassion of my heart,
Step off your merry-go-round! . . .

O when will you start *being* the church; . . .
stop making the church a place to go to,
   and make it something to be;
stop building churches,
   and start being the Kingdom of God in the midst?

A Sunday-school teacher and a minister asked me for copies; the teacher wanted to use the paraphrase in her next lesson. (The complete quotation follows, under the heading CHURCH.)

With such things I have tried to fill this book. Everything here was chosen to light up or underscore or bring more of the breath of life to what you want to communicate. Most of it will be most useful if it appeals to you enough to become so much a part of yourself that you can see and feel it and put it into your own words and your hearers' hearts.

When Clarence Jordan made his inimitable translation of the Acts of the Apostles, the title came out "Happenings." There are happenings every day that underscore all kinds of moral principles and spiritual insights and prove that God is very much alive and active on our planet.

To the best of my knowledge, nothing in this book is anemic from overexposure and repetition. Nearly everything is from the events, books, periodicals, films, and ideas of 1969 and 1970. In most cases the material is followed by questions, included to provoke thought and discussion, and in some cases I have added Scripture references that seemed pertinent.

The illustrations are arranged alphabetically by topic, with built-in cross-references and further cross references in the index at the end of the book. At the end there is also a list of sources of material for teaching and discussion, and a list of periodicals that strike me as especially valuable gold mines of current illustrations.

This book is for you. Please let me know if it helps you, and how I can make the next volume better.

D.T.K.

CONTENTS

7

ALCOHOL AND COMMON SENSE

In the novel (and motion picture) *True Grit* by Charles Portis, teen-age Mattie Ross is offered a drink of whiskey for her cold by the hard-bitten federal marshal Rooster Cogburn, to whom whiskey is no stranger. Mattie says, "I would not put a thief in my mouth to steal my brains."

Van Nostrand's Scientific Encyclopedia, published in 1968, says of alcohol:

"Contrary to lay opinion, it is not a stimulant, but a depressant. . . . Careful tests have shown that alcohol does not increase either the mental or physical abilities. It is the psychic effect of the drug which results in the individual's estimation of his own performance as greatly improved whereas, actually, his mental reaction time and manual skill are decreased."

No doubt Mattie Ross had observed the slowed-down mental and physical reactions, the slurred speech and the ludicrous movements of those who had imbibed too much alcohol. She had common sense, and science confirms her instincts.

Why do so many young people today have no interest in following their elders' examples in drinking? Does the young person have a point who says to his parent, "Why do you bug me about pot when you couldn't get along without your cocktails and pills?" What is the best antidote to alcohol addiction? What does the Bible have to say about this problem?

For reference: Proverbs 20:1; 23:20–21; 31:4–5; Matthew 26:27–29; Romans 13:13–14.

ALCOHOLISM

"If alcoholism were a communicable disease, a national emergency would be declared."—Dr. William C. Menninger.

"The National Council on Alcoholism states that of all the illnesses which affect family life, none is more devastating than alcoholism."—*The Catholic News,* March 27, 1969.

The four major threats to health in America today are cancer, heart disease, mental illness, and alcoholism. Much effort is being put into the fight against the first three. What should we be doing about the fourth?

See also DRINKING AND DRIVING.

ALIENATION OF YOUTH

In his book *Not Quite So Simple* Senator Mark O. Hatfield has a sympathetic word for young people, who are often condemned today:

"Youth's alienation and rejection of traditional forms of authority have been magnified by the Vietnam war. Interpreted by an older generation as lacking in patriotism, these young men who question our commitment in the war are often motivated by the highest form of love for their country and the principles upon which it was founded."

Do you agree or disagree? It has been said that there is always some degree of alienation between the generations. Is this true? Is there an extra dimension to the "alienation gap" today? If so, does the war in Vietnam have something to do with it?

If youth are alienated by us who are older, what can or should we do about it—if anything? Should we put the discontented young people, who are sons and daughters of some of us, behind bars until they think like us? Which is better: denouncing or trying to understand? Is it possible that some things that belong to the older generation should be changed?

See also PATRIOTISM, WAR, YOUNG PEOPLE.

Sometimes it is good to see ourselves as others see us, particularly when they can reassure us and keep us headed toward the goals we need.

When the National Commission on the Causes and Prevention of Violence reported later in 1969, it startled many Americans with its conclusion that we face greater danger from our own lust for violence than from anything abroad. This is the studied conclusion of some very able men, and we ought not to be quick to reject it.

But we may also profit from a Britisher's view of America today. One chapter of the report is by Louis Heren, the Washington correspondent for *The Times* of London, and is entitled "The Strengths of America."

One of the strengths: *our age as a nation*. Politically, Heren points out, we are the second oldest country in the world; our political system has been functioning longer than that of any country except Great Britain. By comparison with most nations, "the United States is a mature, almost ancient land, made immensely stable by established tradition."

Another strength: *our unity*. While continental Europe seems hopelessly divided politically and even economically, America has integrated immigrants from all kinds of cultures and backgrounds into a single union.

Third: *our capacity for successful change*. "Americans," says Heren, "should be amazed by their capacity to accept change with a minimum of violence." While there are tremendous strains between the French and English sections of Canada and the Protestant and Catholic loyalties of Ireland, we have overcome many such tensions and been flexible enough to adapt to changing conditions without breaking.

"If there is an American dream," writes Heren, "the one distinction (for most men dream) is that Americans can hope to realize their dreams regardless of race, color, and creed."

Can we build on these strengths to make our dreams come true?

It is written: "And it shall come to pass in the last days, saith God, I will pour out my Spirit upon all flesh: and your sons and your daughters shall prophesy, and your young men shall see visions, and your old men shall dream dreams" (Acts 2:17).

AMERICA: God's Country?

A plaque used in the vacation school program of one church contains the words "God's Country" adjoining a map of the United States. Many of us have at times referred to our favorite part of the good earth as "God's Country" a bit facetiously, but does the United States have a special place in God's heart?

Yes—along with every other country on this planet. In the January 30, 1970, issue of *Christianity Today,* John Warwick Montgomery says he can stand the unsolicited invitations he gets in the mail to join a Bunny Club, but what he has difficulty tolerating is the rightist propaganda that assumes the U.S.A. is uniquely "God's Country" and that the founding fathers of this nation were conservative Christians. The fathers, he points out, ranged from Franklin the freethinker to Thomas Paine the deist. Furthermore:

"In reality, ours is no more 'God's Country' than is any other part of this sin-impregnated globe. We are not the Israelite theocracy repristinated, nor are we the pinnacle of Christian civilization. What we have accomplished positively as a nation is due, not to ourselves, but to God's grace. And for our Hiroshimas and My Lai massacres we stand under the wrath of the Almighty just as others do for their Pearl Harbors and Buchenwalds. Perhaps the judgment against us is even greater, 'for unto whomsoever much is given, of him shall much be required.' "

The statement, "He hath not dealt so with any nation" (Psalm 147:20), is sometimes applied to this country. Truly God has dealt wonderfully with us. But the Psalmist was

20

referring, of course, to ancient Israel, and every nation might apply the statement to its own protection and preservation.

Does America have any special claim on God's grace? Whose country is this? Do we have any responsibility to people of other countries? What?

AMERICA: Politics and Power

"The only thing America respects is power."—Allan Fagan, Jr.

When Mr. Fagan, a New York political leader, said that to a voters' group, there were many angry expressions of disagreement. How true is it? What place has power had in American history?

AMERICA: What Are Our Priorities?

"Perhaps the usual discussion of national priorities is too abstract, or is largely seen by middle-class power-holders as aimed at benefiting the other fellow. Consider, then, a specific fact. Dr. Sidney Farver, past-president of the American Cancer Society, believes: 'We are so close to a cure for cancer. We lack only the will and the kind of money and comprehensive planning that went into putting a man on the moon.'

"As the Citizens' Committee for the Conquest of Cancer has been pointing out in national advertising, more than 318,000 Americans died of cancer last year. At the same time, the United States spent more every day on military affairs than we spend in a year on cancer research. The goal suggested by the Committee is at once simple and breathtaking: an all-out drive to try to conquer cancer by America's two-hundredth birthday. What a great way to celebrate! On the other hand, if there is no new cure, one out of four Americans now alive, 51,000,000 people, will suffer from cancer of some sort; one out of six, 34,000,000 people, will die of cancer. The next time there is discussion of your tax dollar and reordering national priorities, you might think of this."[1]

Is what we call defense so much more important than finding the cure for cancer? What should a Christian nation put first? What are our personal priorities? What should they be?

AMERICA: Which Way?

The whole back page of the *National Register* for January 25, 1970, was a poster. The top half showed half an American eagle, olive branch in claw; the bottom half, almost a mirror image of the top, showed the same eagle brandishing a spear. Between the two halves of the schizophrenic eagle appeared the ancient words: "And if a house is divided against itself, that house cannot stand . . . If a kingdom is divided against itself, that kingdom cannot stand."

Jesus said it, and Abraham Lincoln quoted it when the Union seemed in danger of dividing. Today America seems divided in many ways, but perhaps it is divided most about its meaning, its purpose, its place in the world. We cannot go in two directions at once. We must choose which way.

"There is a new America every morning," Adlai Stevenson once said. ". . . It is upon us whether we will it or not. The New America is the sum of many small changes . . . that add up to a broad transformation of our lives. Our task is to guide these changes. For though change is inevitable, change for the better is a full-time job."

Which is better: to drift with the tide, or to swim (either against the tide or with it) to get somewhere? To look at change fatalistically, or to work for the best?

The *National Register* commented about its poster: "It speaks not only of the important decisions made by leaders in legislative halls, but of the small changes in values and attitudes that take place each day in the minds and hearts of the

[1] *Commonweal*, February 13, 1970. Used by permission.

American people—changes that move the nation slowly but inexorably in the direction either of life or of death."

What kind of nation do we want? What are we doing— either positively or by doing nothing and letting other forces fill the vacuum of our inaction—to make our country truly great?

AMERICA AND THE FUTURE

This nation is one of the unquestioned leaders of the world in power and influence. What will or should our role be in the future?

Recently, Cardinal Cushing of Boston said: "In the Sixties we discovered that peace is an idea whose time has come . . . The Seventies must be a time when nations will turn outlays for weapons systems into outlays for food, education, medicine, economic development—the vital ingredients for a viable peace. We have discovered we were a people gone astray. The traumatic repetition of acts of violence compel us to search our individual and collective consciences as we have rarely done before."

It has been said that America has given more money unselfishly to other countries than any other nation in history. Do we have any obligation to continue? How does the proportion of our gross national product devoted to foreign aid compare with that of other countries? Does America have a national purpose? What is it? What is the best way to insure that a world of freedom, peace, and the pursuit of happiness is possible for our children?

AMERICA AND THE WORLD

"We own half the trucks in the world. We own almost half of all the radios in the world. We own a third of all the electricity that's produced in the world.

"And although we have only about 6 percent of the population in the world, we have half its wealth. And bear in mind, that other 94 percent of the population all would like to trade with us.

"Now I would like to see them enjoy the blessings that we enjoy. But don't you help them exchange places with us because I don't want to be where they are."[1]

Does this wealth, in proportion to the rest of the world's poverty, obligate us to do anything about the three billion individuals who have so little? Why do Americans have half the earth's trucks and radios and riches? How much of all this would we have without the oil and rubber and metals we get from the Middle East, Southeast Asia, and various other parts of the world? Is it fair to other nations to create a balance of trade that results in their growing poverty and our multiplying wealth?

For reference: John 3:16; Leviticus 19:9–18; Amos 4:1–3; 5:11–24; James 2:1–17.

AMERICAN FOREIGN AID

Every year the United States gives away millions of dollars in foreign aid. While some citizens point with pride to their country's generosity in helping other countries, others say that most of the aid is used to bolster the military and business interests of this nation. And other nations may be doing more than we are.

A release in December, 1969, from the American Baptist News Service began, "Japan may be the first developed industrial nation to reach the goal in foreign aid of 1 percent of its gross national product." The World Bank has set a goal of 1 percent for the developed nations to reach by 1975, and Japan is well on its way toward that goal.

Meanwhile, America is decreasing its foreign aid; in 1969,

[1] Former President Lyndon B. Johnson in a speech to the Junior Chamber of Commerce, June 28, 1967.

Congress suggested an amount totaling less than one half of 1 percent of the United States' gross national product. Which leaves America in a position similar to the church member who boasts about how much he gives to his church, while his poorer neighbor gives twice the percentage of his income.

Should a nation, as well as an individual, practice philan-thropy and good-neighbor relationships toward other countries? Could this be a form of stewardship? If we are a nation under God, do we have a responsibility toward the other members of the family of nations?

See also FOREIGN AID, INTERNATIONAL RELATIONSHIPS, PA-TRIOTISM.

AMERICAN INDIANS AND OUR TEXTBOOKS

The fourth-grade social-science reader *Exploring New England* by Harold B. Clifford, published by Follett Publishing Company in Chicago, carries this inspiring account of how a company of New England soldiers led by Captain John Mason responded to the "threat" of a tribe of Pequot Indians. In the textbook, this is how a boy named Robert hears the story of the white men's attack:

"His little army attacked in the morning before it was light and took the Pequots by surprise. The soldiers broke down the stockade with their axes, rushed inside, and set fire to the wigwams. They killed nearly all the braves, squaws, and children, and burned their corn and other food. There were no Pequots left. . . .

" 'I wish I were a man and had been there,' thought Robert."

Is this the way the children in your community are learning history and citizenship? For many years the white men who massacred most of this country's natives, taught them how to scalp human beings, gave them whiskey, took their land, and broke countless treaties with them, looked on those original Americans as vile, worthless beasts. Today we know the truth: that the first Americans worshiped the Great Spirit who created the world, that they saved the lives of the first settlers and fought back only after ceaseless betrayals and massacres such as that of the Pequots. *But are our children learning the truth? Is murdering women and children something to admire and emulate?*

APPLYING CHRISTIANITY: "The Christian Position"?

A religious periodical advertises itself as a journal with "clear, candid statements of the Christian position on even the most controversial issues." Some of us believe emphatically that Christians ought to take a stand on important issues, even at the risk of choosing the wrong stand. But we are not convinced that we can call what *we* think is right "the Christian position." There are too many Christians taking another stance entirely. Does this mean we are moral agnostics, unable to arrive at a Christian position? Not at all. We have to arrive at our position on the basis of the Bible, the life and teachings of Jesus, and the meaning of Christianity. We believe that we have found a Christian position. But we are unwilling to tell everyone else off, or to suggest that the other fellow's position is sub- or anti-Christian. We must stand where we must, but we try to make allowance for the other guy's sincerity, for his own right to reach a different conclusion. We may not agree with him, but we hesitate to imply that the only Christian position is ours.

Should Christians take a stand on controversial issues? On nonreligious issues? What makes a problem religious? Should some matters be left to the scientists, the educators, the generals, the politicians? Is Christ Lord of only the church, or Lord of all?

See also CHRISTIANITY, CHURCH.

ASTROLOGY AND THE FUTURE

Every so often a self-styled prophet or astrologer appears to make an accurate prediction about something, but did you ever notice how often the seers strike out? At the end of 1968, "Penultimate" pointed out in the January 21, 1970, *Christian Century,* a number of psychics committed themselves to predictions about what would happen in 1969.

Joseph DeLouise wrote in the Chicago *Sun-Times* that Johnny Carson's contract would not be renewed (it was), a type of birth control would be found that would be acceptable to the church fathers (it wasn't), and "Neither Russia nor the United States will put a man on the moon in 1969." (1969, you recall, happened to be the year that four American astronauts walked on the surface of Luna.)

In the same paper Henry Y. Dutton said that peace would be achieved in 1969, and both Irene F. Hughes and "Harriet" said flatly that the United States would not get a man to the moon.

But 1969 is not an exception. And professional psychics aren't the only ones who fall flat on their forecasts. Just before the Japanese attack on Pearl Harbor in December 1941, *Look* magazine published the predictions of nine of America's smartest observers of world affairs. Commentator Raymond Clapper said, "Japan will be checked by military and economic pressure." Journalist Edgar Snow said, "Japan cannot effectively attack" the United States. Major George Fielding Eliot said, "Japan will be swiftly and decisively beaten." CBS broadcaster Henry Flannery said, "Possibly in the fall the United States will issue a declaration of war." None of the nine forecasters gave any inkling of what would happen about the time *Look* hit the newsstands. While these predictions were being printed, Japan's fleet was on its way to Pearl Harbor.

Religious people also, however, have the bad habit of predicting futures that don't happen. In 1921 William E. Blackstone wrote down his calculations for the end of the world and came out with this conclusion: "This gives us a period of sixteen years from 1917 to 1933, which appears to be the *TIME OF THE END.*" (Capitals and italics are Blackstone's.) He went on to describe what would happen in those sixteen years: the rebuilding of the temple in Jerusalem, the establishment of the Antichrist and the battle of Armageddon, with the destruction of the Gentile governments of the world. A respected church group published Blackstone's predictions.

Are we here to figure out the future or to bring about God's will in the present? Is the Bible "history written in advance" or something different?

For reference: Mark 13:32; Acts 1:7; Luke 19:13.

AUTHORITY IN THE CHURCH: What and Where Is It?

Jacqueline Grennan Wexler symbolizes all that is happening in present-day religious and intellectual life. For twenty years she was hidden away from the world, a nun of the Sisters of Loretto. She got permission from the Pope to make experimental changes in the order, then left it to concentrate on serving as president of Webster College. This was a Catholic school which became news when Sister Jacqueline got it under control of a non-Catholic board. Late in 1969 she married and became president of Hunter College in New York City, where she will probably keep things moving in unforeseeable new directions.

The big thing that is changing in religion today is authority —which is being shaken as never before. Authority Mrs. Wexler sees as one of the prime issues today[1]:

"I am convinced that institutional religion can and should no longer exercise any regulatory authority over its own membership, and certainly no such regulatory authority over the full human family. Precisely because its role is spiritual, because it frankly is interested in the formation of conscience and life style, institutional religion must cease confusing the control of behavior decree with the power of persuasion in gaining intellectual assent. The really great teacher is effective in dealing with mature students by conveying to them their right to accept all, part, or none of his thesis. We are beginning to realize

[1] Reprinted by special permission of *Ladies' Home Journal*, © 1969 by Downe Publishing, Inc.

28

that a teacher's effectiveness is equally dependent on his ability to convey his own realization of the unfinished and imperfect state of his own theories. Great authors speak with authority because they are honestly searchers after truth, makers of new clarity, provocateurs of new questions. Theirs is always a prophetic role. To the degree that the author, the teacher and the master must play an honest part in regulating the behavior of the students, he is not *at the same time* and *within the same domain* free to manifest the role of seeker, clarifier, provocateur.

"As the institutional churches elect or are forced to abdicate the power to regulate behavior, they are freed to exercise their essential prophetic mission; they can speak with authority in man's continuing search for meaning in his personal and social world. Revealed truths are basic insights subject to extension, elaboration and clarification by their interaction with new 'truths' and new insights. Within this perspective, denominational religions are working groups brought and held together by common heritage and/or common function, sharing their insights with all other secular and religious groups and provoking each other in the continuing search for clarity. If religious denominations see themselves as ideologists instead of sharing searchers after truth, they become defenders of their investments rather than explorers of their faith."

The churches no longer have the power they once had in the world; Jacqueline Grennan Wexler says it's a good thing! Do you agree? Would you like to see religion have more or less control over:

1. *Who may marry whom,*
2. *The right to birth-control information,*
3. *What a person believes,*
4. *The beliefs of political figures,*
5. *People's personal lives?*

That list could be extended much further, but it suggests where some of the concern is and has been among those who dissent.

Religious authority has been a divisive force in the world

for centuries. Even today, many Protestants resent the attempts of some Catholics to legislate on matters like birth control, while many Catholics are fearful of practices in school and government that in their view are really Protestant. Many Jews, meanwhile, fear that Christians may return to the attitudes that kept Jews out of certain businesses, out of public office, out of whole countries—unless they forsook their faith.

Is Mrs. Wexler correct in saying that if the churches had less external power, they would be freed for their real mission? What is their mission? Worldly or spiritual? External or internal?

One other point: teaching. *Do you agree that a great teacher or author is effective not because he claims a special authority, but because of his honest dedication to truth and the search for it?* When Jesus taught, it is recorded that people were astonished, "for he taught them as one that had authority, and not as the scribes" (Mark 1:22).

People of Jesus' time were accustomed to religious teachers who made a great show of claiming to have the authority of God, and therefore expected everyone to do what they said. They were surprised because Jesus' authority was different. *How? Do you suppose it was not in some external authority he claimed, but that the truth was obvious, convincing, in his words themselves?*

How could this apply to good teaching today? To witnessing about our faith?

AUTOMATION AND IMPERSONALITY: The Anderson Tapes

In the book *The Anderson Tapes* by Lawrence Sanders, one listens in as the Mafia plots a major crime. The FBI records bits and pieces of the plotters' conversations through wire taps and hidden microphones and various "bugs." So does the Federal Trade Commission. So do the Securities and Exchange Commission, the Internal Revenue Service, and other federal agencies. The story unfolds through the federal eavesdroppers' tapes and records; the Mafia's plans go forward, and one watches with mounting horror as the crime is about to take place.

But each spy, each federal agency keeps the information to himself or itself. The SEC is interested only in whether there is any violation of stock sales; the IRS, only in whether the plotters are avoiding their income tax. Nothing else is the personal concern of the official listener!

Isn't this a perfect example of the absurdities our automated, bureaucratized, impersonal civilization can lead to? One concern of a number of church and government leaders today is the reversal of such depersonalization, the breaking down of artificial walls, the return of common sense and personal responsibility to our mechanized culture. What can you and I do about this? Should we return to a simpler way of life? Or should we accept the values of our technology and try to work with God to make good servants of those processes and forces which may otherwise master us? Or should we include both of these approaches among the options with which we as Christians face the future?

THE BIBLE: Where Are the Words?

In her book *Only One Year*, Stalin's daughter, Svetlana Alliluyeva, recounts the experiences that led her from the emptiness of atheism in Russia to faith and freedom in America. In the spring of her thirty-fifth year, Svetlana began to be aware of God's presence in nature and of the reality of the invisible, spiritual world. Happiness filled her soul to the brim. She writes:

"I looked for the words that could express this new sensation, and found it in the Psalms of David. Since then I have known nothing that better expressed the Higher, Eternal Life, immense, filling the whole Universe, to which my small life belonged like a tiny speck of dust. . . .

"Nowhere have I found words more powerful than those in the Psalms. Their fervid poetry cleanses one, gives one strength, brings hope in moments of darkness. Makes one look critically into oneself, convict oneself, and wash one's heart clean with one's own tears. It is the ever-burning fire of love, of gratitude, humility, and truth."

We might not express it in just those words—but isn't this a remarkable statement of appreciation of Scripture by a former atheist? Does the Bible mean as much to us? Do we find in it vision, power, cleansing, love, truth? If not, why not? If so, could we share our admiration and witness as convincingly as the daughter of Stalin has done?

THE BIBLE AND YOUNG PEOPLE

Two Lutheran ministers who came to New York saw something in Greenwich Village they could hardly believe. Two hippies, they later told John Erickson of the American Bible Society, were looking at a copy of the Society's new translation, *Good News for Modern Man,* on a street corner. One of the two was heard to mutter, "Looks like the Bible, man, but it can't be. I dig it!"

Unfortunately, to many people the Bible is a book of archaic words and unintelligible phrases. A modern translation is unrecognizable as Scripture. Yet Jesus spoke in the language of the ordinary people of Galilee, and the New Testament was written in the common garden-vegetable Greek of the Roman world. There is no reason for the Bible to remain buried in the dead language of past centuries. The great virtue of the new translations is that young people dig them.

See also NUCLEAR DESTRUCTION AND THE BIBLE, SCRIPTURE, TROUBLE AND HOPE, YOUNG PEOPLE.

BLACK AND WHITE: The Other Fellow's Shoes

In *The Prince and the Pauper* Mark Twain shows how easily clothes and circumstances make the man. The Prince of England changes clothes and positions with a boy of the streets, and learns for the first time what it is like to be poor and helpless at the bottom of a great society. After he gets back to his throne, the Prince has a new interest in justice and decent conditions for the unfortunate.

Notre Dame University's president, Rev. Theodore Hesburgh, says: "If you were caught in the web of poor education, lack of economic opportunity, . . . poor housing and degraded neighborhoods, shamed a dozen times a day because whatever your quality as a person you could not eat or rest or sleep where others can—if this were your lot, would you cry: 'Freedom now'? And would you consider this impatience if your cry came a hundred years after you had been declared free?"

Would you?

BLACKS AND HOPE: Raisin in the Sun

What happens to a dream deferred?

Does it dry up
like a raisin in the sun?
Or fester like a sore—
and then run?
Does it stink like rotten meat?
Or crust and sugar over—
like a syrupy sweet?

Maybe it just sags
like a heavy load.

Or does it explode?

So asked the gifted black poet Langston Hughes in "Harlem."[1] How many black people for how many generations have longed to have decent homes, decent jobs, a decent education, equal justice, equal treatment? *If the black dream is the Amer-*

---

[1] Copyright 1951 by Langston Hughes. Reprinted from *The Panther and the Lash* by Langston Hughes, by permission of Alfred A. Knopf, Inc.

ican dream of justice and freedom, what does *happen when the
dream remains unfulfilled? Is it strange if it finally explodes?
How would I like it if my children had to live in an apartment
full of rats, and powerful white people would not let me move
out? Is the church right or wrong when it tries to do something
about such things? What should it be doing—anything?*

See also RACE RELATIONS.

BOOKS AND CIVILIZATION

One of the important battles of today, Dr. Mason Gross,
president of Rutgers University and chairman of the National
Book Committee, told a library group, is the battle between
books and television. Television presents a tremendous emotional
impact, but a picture does not present a clear thought. Television
depends upon an instant response, but you cannot turn your
set back to go over what was said three minutes back. Television
is making us descend "into something like the global village
that Mr. Marshall McLuhan warns us about, where there will
be no more sharpness or elegance to the life of human beings,
but instead a great big blob of emotional reactions. This must
never be."

The only alternative, says Dr. Gross, is the printed word,
the reading and thinking about what is written in books and
periodicals. Books give us the tools with which to think, to
resist the dehumanization of language and the remaking of
words into propaganda. "So, for the sake of analysis, for the
sake of reason, for the sake of study, for the sake of reflection,
we've simply got to bring our kids and ourselves away from
the television sets occasionally and back to books."

*Do you agree? What can television do that books can't?
What can books do that television can't? Must television threaten
reading, or can it encourage it? What part do written words
play in a business organization? A government? A religion?
Would our faith be the same without the Bible? Do we make
adequate use of that?*

BOREDOM AND DESPAIR: Why?

Many people today seem bored, fatalistic, uncertain that there is anything good in the future. In James Gould Cozzens' novel *Morning Noon and Night,* Henry Dodd Worthington sees himself as the product of blind accidents, his life "little governed by logic or demonstrable cause and effect," a game of blind man's buff. Ahead he sees "thin final sunlight" before "the child must . . . be taken away to bed." Bertrand Russell once said that man's life is "a curious accident in a backwater" of the universe.

In his book *Apology for Wonder,* Dr. Sam Keen says that modern man has lost a sense of God, and life has shriveled. "When every present moment is the inevitable outcome of the past, the sense of astonishment and adventure are replaced by weariness, boredom and finally despair."

How can we recover zest? Will religion alone do it? One young man decided to become a priest because, he said, "All the priests I knew looked happy." What is the secret of real happiness? Someone has defined "blessedness" as "happiness with its roots in eternity." Where are our roots?

BROTHERHOOD

A short while ago we learned that a neighbor of ours, Milt Peters, had suffered $19,000 worth of damage from a fire in his kitchen. When we asked whether we could do anything to help, Milt said with feeling, "Thanks, but everyone in our church has offered to take care of the children, to have us in for meals, and they've already given us so much clothing that we have at least three times as much as we lost in the fire.

"I never knew what Christian brotherhood was before," Milt went on. "I never would have believed so many people cared so much—people we didn't know at all, but now we know they're for real. I never did go for this hypocrites-in-the-church bit, and this proves to me that Christians really put their hearts where their mouths are."

Do you suppose that a lot of church members don't take more social action because they have never been sufficiently challenged by a clear and present opportunity? Is it possible that all of us need to open our eyes and hearts to the needs around us? Is brotherhood demonstrated simply by putting money in an envelope? Does religion sometimes miss out on the personal touch, in which Jesus excelled? If brotherhood doesn't begin in the church, where can it begin? What did Jesus say about his brothers and sisters?

For reference: Mark 3:35; Matthew 25:40; James 2:15; I John 2:10; 3:10; 3:14, 17; 4:20.

See also CHRISTIANITY, CHURCH, UNITY IN THE CHURCH.

BROTHERHOOD AND BACTERIAL WARFARE

The Illinois Institute of Technology Research Institute is engaged in a military research study of "aerosol dissemination of infectious microorganisms, particularly of Venezuelan equine encephalomyelitis and Q-fever rickettsiae."

It has been reported that the bacterial weapons the United States Government has already stockpiled could kill everyone on earth many times over. How many more poisons do we need?

BROTHERLY LOVE: Rhetoric or Action?

"New York—The blacks who wrote and support the Black Manifesto 'hear' church members' behavior rather than their official message of brotherly love, and their perception is deeply theological, a leading commentator said here.

"He is Dr. Gerhard Wiebe, dean of the School of Public

Communication, Boston University, and he spoke at a consultation of some one hundred church media experts, called to study the communication problems raised by the manifesto."[1]

Which means more—what a politician says or what he does? Which means more to those around us—what we Christians say or what we do? What do we really think about black people? Is there any question that they know this, rather than what we sometimes say in official church statements?

Someone has said that the white Southern attitude toward black people is, "Come as near us as you like but don't you get too high," while white Northerners say to them, "Go as high as you can but don't come too near." Is this true? If you were a white minority in a colored world, how would you like to be treated? The time may come soon when the colored majority wakes up, realizes it is in the majority, and begins treating whites the way whites treated non-whites for centuries. Meanwhile, what is our attitude toward those who are not white?

BUSINESS AND BUNNIES

A gasoline station in New Jersey uses girls in scanty bunny costumes to boost sales. A shoe-store chain in New York employs "harem girls" to sell shoes. "We think the more skin showing, the more sales," the owner told a reporter. Picturing one of the barefoot harem girls, the *Record* of December 3, 1969, commented, "more and more businesses are using scantily clad girls to sell merchandise."

Whayne Eisenman, an Associated Press writer, interviewed the president of a trade-show promotion firm who said, "Some very high caliber drug firms have asked us for topless and nude girls to promote products at medical seminars." Somehow it's not as surprising to hear of topless waitresses at restaurants and bars in California as to learn that nudity sells drugs to

[1] News release from United Methodist Information, January 30, 1970.

doctors. Columnist Nicholas von Hoffman says he got a lot of angry complaints from physicians for pointing out that drug companies use pictures of naked or near-naked girls in their ads in medical magazines. In a column in the Washington *Post* of November 26, 1969, entitled "Drug Ads," Von Hoffman quoted the testimony of Dr. Edward R. Pinckney, a former editor of the Journal of the American Medical Association. Pinckney said that the Journal found that its demands for proof of its advertisers' claims decreased the advertising, and the screening of ads virtually stopped. Misleading statements were published without correction, said Dr. Pinckney: "Although the A.M.A. claimed to have 'advertising principles,' such principles never really existed in fact."

Dr. Pinckney is a past chairman of preventive medicine at Northwestern University and has written more than a hundred articles and editorials in medical journals. It is deeply shocking to find such a man stating that drug companies are relying on bare skin rather than medical facts to sell doctors their products, and that medical journals permit erroneous or misleading advertisements to lure busy physicians to buy their drugs.

Comments Nicholas von Hoffman, "Nobody knows how many people die or are hospitalized or how much money is spent or pain endured because a doctor prescribes a drug he shouldn't have."

Using beautiful flowers, cars, or girls to sell merchandise is fine—if it doesn't replace honesty and truth. When anyone puts his own profits ahead of someone else's life or well-being, however, Christians must protest.

And what about the girls who are so generously "used" today? What does it do to their self-esteem to learn that to many men they are nothing more than bait—as valuable as a throwaway handbill?

And what does all this say about you and me when we let hucksters "use" human beings to get our dollars, and fall into their flesh traps?

Soon, says Whayne Eisenman, "sex and the single salesgirl might become as American as apple pie." Will they? Will you and I help make it happen?

BUSINESS AND ETHICS: "Churning" Bertha Hecht

Most of her life Bertha Hecht worked as a housekeeper for no more than $125 a month. Born in England, she served one American employer so faithfully that he married her and left her more than half a million dollars. Bertha left the money with her investor, and between that time and seven years later, while the stock market was zooming to amazing new heights, her investments fell to a worth of about a quarter of a million dollars.

She sued the investment firm—one of Wall Street's respected brokerage houses. Early in 1970 the court ruled that Mrs. Hecht had been defrauded and awarded her $375,000. It also took note that:

1. About a third of all the commodity commissions at the brokerage office branch which served Mrs. Hecht came from transactions involving the widow's funds.

2. Nearly two thirds of all the commodity commissions of her agent came from her transactions.

3. The firm charged Mrs. Hecht nearly $200,000 for commissions and mark-ups.

4. While Mrs. Hecht's stocks were dwindling to less than half their original value, the original value of her portfolio increased to more than a million dollars. In other words, if this widow had done nothing at all with her stocks, they would have doubled in value.

Robert Metz, reporting this incident in the New York *Times* of February 14, 1970, called it "churning." Some of us might say that Mrs. Hecht was "creamed" or "cleaned out," or we might be tempted to use very inelegant words to describe what happened.

39

Did those involved think what they did would never come to light because the victim was a foreigner, aged, and a widow? Did they think she would not know what they were doing? or that she was so unused to money that she would not miss losing a few hundred thousands?

No doubt such instances are rare. How can they be kept at or reduced to a minimum? What responsibility does a business firm have toward its clients? One company habitually made punctual payments to people it considered important or influential, but habitually paid late those it thought would never tell. How widespread is the tendency to cut as many corners as you can get away with? Are most people decent and honorable, or not? Does the proportion matter, as far as our own values are concerned? Do we need new business ethics, or will the old ones do? How do we know what is right?

BUSINESS AND ETHICS: One Company's Applied Christianity

Jan Erteszek is an amazing individual. After Hitler's conquest of Poland, he and his wife were among the penniless refugees of Europe. They walked from Poland clear across Europe, seldom knowing where they were, where they would get their next meal, or how. Today Mr. Erteszek is president of the Olga Company, one of America's finest lingerie manufacturers. He founded it with ten dollars and a "deep commitment to fulfilling the needs of people." Today the company does over fourteen million dollars' worth of business a year.

In February 1970, Mr. Erteszek told members of the Laymen's Movement at a New York luncheon meeting how he applies his faith in Christ to his business. One thing to which he is committed is profit sharing; not less than 20 percent of the Olga Company's annual profits are shared with all the employees, so that everyone in the firm is rewarded for company success. Then, there is an open-door relationship with every employee. If a worker has a problem or grievance he is encouraged to take it up with his supervisor, but President Erteszek insists that the worker come to him if he is not satisfied —and he tries to make it easy for this to happen. Another attempt to bring Christianity into the business is at the point of a worker's termination with the company. If a man is let go, he is told what the firm thinks his weaknesses are, but he is not fired. The worker is kept on the payroll until he finds another job.

"I know how hard it is to find work if you're not already employed," said the president, and he sounded as though he spoke from the empathy of experience.

The Olga Company also works actively to bring in minority employees. A branch in Mexico is making an impact on the community where it hires local residents, and there is another in the United States near an Indian reservation.

What do you think of these principles? Are some of them merely good business? Must there be a conflict between business and Christianity? In what other ways do you think a company might put Christianity into practice? What are the responsibilities of the employees? of the customers?

See also TRUTH AND BUSINESS, TRUTH IN ADVERTISING.

CAPITALISM AND CARS

A mailing from an agency trying to prove that capitalism is better than communism, lists the products of the U.S.A. vs. those of the U.S.S.R.: over seventy-five million cars here against less than a million there, over ninety-three million telephones here to less than eight million there.

I happen to prefer capitalism to communism, but not because of such comparisons. I'm not convinced that having more cars than someone else proves much of anything except that one has more cars than the other. Besides, what good are all those cars when they're jammed end to end in traffic jams, roasting the occupants in the summer and in winter filling their lungs with carbon monoxide? What good are all those telephones when all you can get are busy signals and wrong numbers? Maybe our traffic and telephone jams will get better, but until they do let's not boast so much about how superior we are. We might even remember these words: "Pride goeth before destruction: and an haughty spirit before a fall" (Proverbs 16:18).

Does any one political system have a corner on God? Which is better, to concentrate on criticizing some other nation, or to try to improve our own? Are the Christians in Russia and China any less our brothers and sisters than those in England and Spain?

CARE AND CONCERN: "They Care"

When the White House was host to more than two hundred inmates of rest homes on Thanksgiving Day, 1969, President Nixon disappeared after welcoming the guests. His wife and two daughters remained throughout the meal in the President's place. Acknowledging his daughters' help on many such occasions, President Nixon told a reporter, "They care about the world, the country, their generation, and each in her own way tries her best to help."[1]

They care. That sums up the attitude of a good many young people today. They care about the war in Vietnam, the pollution that is destroying the air and water and life of America, the urban rot that must be reversed, the erosion of moral values, the mechanization and depersonalization of modern life. Most young people don't want to become numbers in computers or cogs in giant machines. They care about life and hope and love—some of them enough to protest against the things they see destroying the ideals they still hold.

It's a great thing to care about the world, the nation, this generation, and the generations to come. It's good that Julie

[1] *Newsweek,* December 8, 1969.

and Patricia feel this way. But they aren't the only ones. Millions of people share their concern.

So does God. The Bible says He "loved the world." He made the Israelites responsible for caring for strangers, feeding the hungry, loving their neighbors as themselves. Part of the record of that may be found in Leviticus 19.

See also CONCERN, JUSTICE AND CHARITY.

CHANGES: Do We Need Them?

Perhaps in response to the bumper stickers that read, "AMERICA—LOVE IT OR LEAVE IT," some automobiles display stickers proclaiming, "AMERICA—CHANGE IT OR LOSE IT." To those who say, "If you don't like it here, get out," others reply, "If we don't keep our country fair to everyone, it won't be America."

The question, however, is: Do we really need any changes? Those who are comfortably settled, or who fear losing what they have, don't want any changes. Those who believe things could be improved, do. Perhaps the comfortable are like the man driving the family car. As he glides along the highway, his teen-age son asks, "Dad, what's that knock in the motor?"

"I don't hear any knock in the motor," says Dad.

"But there is one," says Son, who has a mechanic's sharp ears. "If we don't stop and get it fixed, we'll be in trouble."

Perhaps some Americans can hear and see things that others are not aware of. One man who believes we need to look and listen is David Ginsburg, who said in a speech in Pittsburgh that there are a number of realities all of us should try to do something about:

"The reality of bad schools which can't teach kids to read in lily-white suburban areas any better than in black center-city ghettos.

"The reality of housing costs which are out of reach of even middle-class professionals, black and white, who now find themselves frightened out of the cities and priced out of the suburbs.

"The reality of crime that creates a terrifying sense of insecurity for all who cannot afford the private security systems that are available only in the 'best neighborhoods.'

"The reality of skyrocketing medical and hospital costs, auto insurance costs, and utility charges.

"The reality of a legal system that alienates everyone it touches except the very rich, who can keep out of its reach.

"The reality of inflation that steals the savings of every working man, without regard to color.

"The reality of a tax system whose highest rewards are reserved for those with the highest incomes."

Do you agree that some of these "realities" are important enough to require some kind of change from what we now have? Do you know anyone who can't buy or build a house because of inflation and excessive mortgage costs? Is your income being stolen through inflation? As this is being written early in 1970, President Nixon is making definite changes in the policies and priorities of the United States. Other changes are being made by Congress and the courts in response to the demands of many people. Which of these changes are good and which are not? What should each of us be doing personally to bring about changes that are important for our fellow men?

CHILDREN: Learning and Living

A certain doctor's office has in public view these anonymously written words:

CHILDREN LEARN WHAT THEY LIVE

If a child lives with criticism, he learns to condemn.
If a child lives with hostility, he learns to fight.
If a child lives with ridicule, he learns to be shy.
If a child lives with shame, he learns to be guilty.
If a child lives with tolerance, he learns to be patient.
If a child lives with encouragement, he learns confidence.

44

If a child lives with praise, he learns to appreciate.
If a child lives with fairness, he learns justice.
If a child lives with security, he learns to have faith.
If a child lives with approval, he learns to like himself.
If a child lives with acceptance and friendship, he learns
to find love in the world.

*Which of these characteristics do you want for your child?
How is he or she progressing toward the goals you desire? Are
you living in such a way that the goals will be reached? If the
words in the doctor's office are true, what difference should
they make in your home? Your church school? Your community? The world? What can you do specifically, this week,
to help a child learn what he should?*

CHOOSING SIDES

"Fresh grapes do not appear at our home any more," said
an editorial in the November 25, 1968, *Presbyterian Outlook.*
"Each of us enjoys eating them, but we have joined the boycott. . . ." The editor explained that his family wanted to
support the attempts of those who were trying to improve the
working and living conditions of the migrant workers of California, through the grape boycott, which aimed at fairer wages
for the workers and better relationships with the employers.
The editorial went on:

"There are two sides to every issue. Even Christians will be
divided . . . but the time does come when those who profess
Christianity must choose sides and be counted. . . ."

Yes, there are two sides to everything. Many Americans do
not sympathize with Cesar Chavez and the National Council
of Churches in their attempts to give the grape workers a
fairer share of America's prosperity. Others do. Those who see
the moral issue of fighting the conditions that produce disease
and delinquency among the workers *must* take a stand.

*Can Christians refuse to take sides on important issues? Is
there room in our faith for sitting on the fence? Jesus once*

said, "He that is not with me is against me." Does this apply to such things as a grape boycott?

Is there a danger of choosing the wrong side of an issue? Is this danger as great as the danger of refusing to get involved?

CHRIST'S APPEAL

"There are people today who, though they disdain the church, Christianity, and religion, have limitless admiration for Jesus Christ, and are ready to listen to what he said, and to what is said about him by persons they have learned to respect."[1]

Is this a clue for personal witnessing? A great many young people have little use for organized religion, but when they find out what Jesus did and said they love him, and are ready to learn who he is. What is this strange appeal of a man who died two thousand years ago? Does anyone seriously think He is dead today? What was it about Jesus that first attracted all kinds of people? What about him is most appealing today?

For reference: John 1:1-14; Mark 1:21-45; John 4:4-42; Luke 15:1-32; John 13:1-20; Luke 23:26-49; Acts 1:1-2:47.

CHRIST'S COMING: Do We Recognize Him When He Comes?

Eight Days that Rocked the World is an excellent book on the meaning of Christianity for our time. In it Wallace Chappell, the author, quotes Jesus' words, "Inasmuch as ye have done it unto the least of these my brethren, ye have done it unto me" (Matthew 25:40). He observes that when we hear the Master's words we may tell him we would gladly have given him our best, but he never came. And He will reply in words perhaps like these:

[1] Dr. John A. Mackay in *Christianity Today,* January 2, 1970.

"I came. You see, I was that Negro you jostled into the gutter. I was that Chinese laundryman to whom you were not even courteous. I was that epileptic you said was a drunkard; and even had I been, would my need have been less? I was that wealthy suburban socialite who needed to be aware that life could have meaning and majesty, but you never told me. I was that despised neighbor, that sinful degenerate, that shameless beggar, but you had no time to give, no cheer to offer, no bread to share. I came—oh, the times I came—but you did not know me."

What is Christ really telling us in the twenty-fifth chapter of Matthew? When and how will he come? In what ways does he come to us now? Bill Milliken says that he went to New York to take Christ there, but he learned that Christ was there already in the love and openness and honesty and generosity of the lives of the people whose lives he had come to change. Through them Christ changed Bill!

See also JESUS.

CHRISTIAN LIFE: Are Ups and Downs Necessary?

Is there a way to overcome the struggles and ups and downs so many of us face in the Christian life? Many devout believers say it is possible to reach a plateau of victory that rises far above such struggles and defeats. In his book *The Balanced Christian Life,* Charles C. Ryrie has a diagram of such a plateau. It is followed by another diagram of the spiritual life which looks more like a chart of Wall Street's Dow-Jones Industrial Average than anything else we can think of. It zigs and zags, flutters up and falls back, although the general movement is forward and upward. Ryrie says this latter untidy-appearing picture is closer to the Christian life as it usually is.

Ryrie's statement seems to fit most of the people we know. It also seems to describe, in our opinion, those characters whose lives the Bible says much about. Peter, for example, had ups and downs before and after his conversion and before and after Pentecost.

Which is more important: rising above failure, or making progress in spite of repeated failures? Is there such a thing as "the normal Christian life"? Would it be more healthy and helpful for all of us if we were more frank about our temptations and sins?

CHRISTIANITY: Personal or Social Gospel?

In the 1960s the churches of America kept polarizing over the nature of their gospel. Some Christians swung wholeheartedly behind those who were trying to do something concrete for blacks, Indians, migrant workers, and the poor, and something definite about such problems as pollution and military destruction. Others turned away in revulsion from the thought of aiding Martin Luther King, James Forman, Cesar Chavez, or the Vietnam protesters, and demanded that their churches stay out of politics and "stick to the gospel."

But many Christians could not see their faith in such terms. Billy Graham's associate Leighton Ford told the Methodist Council of Evangelism at Charlotte, North Carolina, in January 1970, that the church must and will get away from the "artificial and unscriptural division between word and deed, the hang-up between personal evangelism on the one hand and social concern on the other." Ernest T. Campbell told his parishioners at Riverside Church in New York that the church must practice both soul-winning and social welfare, but that it must move beyond both into the area of radical social action; that it must not only help patch up society's accident victims, but press for the kind of roads, cars, and laws that will slow down the destruction.

What is the church's mission? How do you and I fit into it? What should we be concerned about most? Does Jesus care whether someone is hungry, or being tortured to death? Do we?

48

CHRISTIANITY: What Is a Christian?

On January 23, 1970, the High Court of Israel decided a question which for some time had perplexed that nation and many Jews and non-Jews throughout the world. Benjamin Shalit is an Israeli naval officer whose wife is French-Scottish. Lieutenant Commander Shalit said that his two children, Oren and Galya, were Jewish. The Israeli Government felt otherwise, since Israeli law prescribed that a Jew must either have a Jewish mother or be a convert to Judaism. So the law said that Oren and Galya were Gentiles, while Lieutenant Commander Shalit said they were Jews. The High Court agreed (five to four) with the lieutenant commander. Henceforth, in Israel, it appears that a Jew is anyone who says he is a Jew.

Long ago the Apostle Paul gave one answer to the question, "Who is a Jew?" "For he is not a real Jew who is one outwardly, nor is true circumcision something external and physical. He is a Jew who is one inwardly and real circumcision is a matter of the heart, spiritual and not literal. His praise is not from men but from God" (Romans 2:28–29). Since the word "Jew" means "He who praises" or "He who is praised," Paul seems to have been going back to the original meaning of the word.

We often say that someone is a Christian. What is a Christian? Is there a difference between people who live in "Christian" countries or have some outward connection with the church, and "real" Christians? What is it? Are we praised by people? Should we be? Do we have a reason for believing we are (or will be) praised by God? Could the government decide who is a Christian? If not, who could? If a "real" Jew is one defined by interior rather than exterior characteristics, in what terms should a Christian be identified?

CHRISTIANITY AND REDEMPTION

Friedrich Schleiermacher was one of the greatest minds of the nineteenth century. His thought and scholarship were devoted to the service of Christ, and his contribution to theology and Biblical criticism still influence the church. Schleiermacher was convinced that the Christian faith is the supreme manifestation of religion, and he explained its eminence in these words:

"Christianity is distinguished from other faiths by the fact that everything in it is related to the redemption accomplished by Jesus."

Everything in our faith radiates from the cross! Christ's ability to make anyone over, to help in any situation, to use even our feeblest efforts toward amazing results, is what the Christian religion is all about.

Another brilliant German thinker, Friedrich Nietzsche, once said, "I would be more ready to believe in the Redeemer if more Christians looked redeemed."

How redeemed do we look in what we do and say? In how many ways does Christ redeem anyone? What is the most important fact about Christianity to you?

CHRISTIANITY AROUND THE WORLD: What's Good About Missions?

The last half of the twentieth century has not been a particularly prestigious time for what used to be called foreign missions. Many countries no longer permit American missionaries to enter. Some of the mistakes and foibles of the mission movement have been exposed, and the very name of missionary is passé in many circles, having been replaced (if at all) with "fraternal worker" or the like. Books such as *The Unpopular Missionary* and *Missionary, Go Home* and *No Graven Image* and *Re-thinking Missions* have "debunked" the whole subject.

So it comes as a pleasant surprise to those Christians who have given much of their time, dollars, and effort to spreading the gospel in other parts of the world, to learn what one of India's leading secular magazines thinks of the mission movement today. In the December 28, 1969, issue of *The Illustrated Weekly of India* there is a section entitled "What India Owes to Christianity." Although at times it raises critical questions, the magazine says:

"Christian endeavor has given India over 150 colleges, 2177 high schools, 214 technical schools and 153 teachers' training schools; 620 hospitals, 670 dispensaries, 86 leprosy centers; 713 orphanages, 87 homes for the aged, 681 hostels and welfare organizations, 275 crèches, 44 agricultural settlements, 27 industrial centers; and several institutions for the blind, the deaf, and the handicapped. What other community has done as much for our country?"

An article by A. Soares says: "The work of missionaries has ranged over the whole spectrum of social welfare, affecting all classes and communities without discrimination, but above all the poorest, the most despised and neglected sections of the people. One would expect due appreciation of the work of missionaries and especially of the spirit of love and dedication they have shown in their work."

Late in 1969 I spent several days in Haiti, that backward Caribbean country between Cuba and the Dominican Republic. The poorest country in Latin America with the greatest hunger and illiteracy and the worst infant mortality rate, Haiti today has one outstanding movement of progress, humanity, and hope: the mission program. I talked to missionaries from various denominations, to businessmen, and to the head of a relief agency. The only group in Haiti that appeared to be doing much about the country's poor food supply, low-protein crops, water shortage, illiteracy, or overpopulation was the Christian community. They—most of them American missionaries—are educating the children, feeding the hungry, providing work for the unemployed, staffing hospitals, supplying information for family planning, experimenting to produce crops and animals for more and better food for all.

Someday the King of Kings will say to those who love him, "I was hungry and you gave me food, I was thirsty and you gave me drink, I was a stranger and you welcomed me, I was naked and you clothed me, I was sick and you visited me, I was in prison and you came to me" (Matthew 25:35–36).

You were there, through your church and your mission giving.

What is right with foreign missions? Why has the missionary endeavor been so criticized? Should any work be exempt from criticism? If criticism is sometimes justified, should we not give honor and praise to whom it is due? Where would you and I be if someone had not come to us or our ancestors and said, "Let me tell you the wonderful good news about Jesus"?

CHRISTIANITY'S ACCOMPLISHMENTS

". . . more has been accomplished in the past twenty years in following Christ's commands to relieve hunger, misery and ignorance than in the previous two thousand . . . in civic morality, in the development and maintenance of human rights (civil, economic and social), the spread of racial and religious tolerance, the aversion to taking human life as vengeance for crime, the revulsion against war as a means of settling national or ideological disputes, and the worldwide determination to eliminate hunger, poverty and disease—our standards of Christian conduct were never higher and our accomplishments never greater."[1]

When there is so much criticism of the church and missions and Christianity, when these all seem so much on the decline, it's good to hear this kind of appreciation of what *has* been accomplished. No doubt our problems are greater than ever before. But perhaps God is waiting to match them against the nerve and will of dedicated haters of everything wrong!

Why do past ages seem better than ours? Are they, really?

[1] Dr. Howard L. Trueman, "Don't Tell *Me* That God Is Dead," *The Observer*, October 15, 1969. Used by permission.

Is there any answer to the question, Is the world getting better or worse?

For reference: Matthew 13:24–30; I Corinthians 15:24–25; Revelation 11:15.

CHURCH: Do We Have to Agree on Everything?

Through much of the history of Protestantism, everyone in a church or denomination had to agree on nearly everything. Dyed-in-the-wool Presbyterians believed that salvation was 100 percent the work of God, while Methodists insisted that man had something to do with it. Both baptized their babies; but Baptists said this was wrong and that baptism meant only immersion, not sprinkling. Then there were all the shades of belief and practice, from the Churches of Christ who insisted that they went purely by the New Testament, to the Episcopalians whose reliance on traditions and on ordination by the right bishops seemed to other Protestants only a hairline away from Catholicism. But even the largest bodies kept splitting up into New Lights and Old Lights, Hardshells and Softshells, High Church and Low Church—sometimes only in mind and attitude, but often dividing into new groups that split and split again.

Early in 1970 Dr. William A. Benfield, minister of First Presbyterian Church in Charleston, West Virginia, said something on this subject that struck us as worth thinking about. Interviewed in *Presbyterian Survey,* he talked about the Consultation on Church Union (in which he is chairman of the Plan of Union Commission), which may result in the reunion of nine major American denominations:

"One of the great things in the plan is recognition that we can belong to the same body without having complete uniformity. This means, therefore, that in the new church, a minister can baptize by sprinkling or immersion, can baptize infants or not, depending on his conscience. These differences therefore do not justify separate denominations."

53

Should they? Isn't it time Christians got together on something more vital than how baptism should be administered, or whether a church is governed by deacons or elders? If we are Christians, shouldn't some of these differences be left up to the individual's conscience, instead of forcing everyone in the church to agree with everyone else on even the most controversial and trivial points?

Many of us no longer think that uniting everyone into one big church will solve our problems. At the moment, we have to live with many different religious groups. Wouldn't it be wonderful if we accepted other people for their life and intentions, and made the same allowances for their faults that we make for our own? If we worked with them in the great causes on which we agree, and stopped worrying so much about the differences?

CHURCH: Has It Lost It?

As Christianity declines on the world scene, Buddhism is making a vigorous comeback. In Japan, the branch of the Buddhist faith known as Soka Gakkai is the fastest-growing religion. In America, Soka Gakkai (or Nichiren Shoshu, as it is known here) has made two hundred thousand converts since 1960.

Some of the adherents of this new faith were pictured in the January 9, 1970, issue of *Life*. Bill Haass, a New York grocer, is quoted as testifying about the Nichiren Shoshu meetings: "Going makes me feel good. . . . Let's face it, the church has lost it. They lost most of my generation and I would say all of the next generation. In church you fall asleep. You don't do that at our meetings. There is too much going on."

Has the church lost the kind of thing the Buddhists have found? If anyone falls asleep in church, why? What is there about Buddhism or yoga or Islam or witchcraft or astrology that seems to give many people today what so many others find in Christianity and the church? Nichiren members invite people

54

off the streets to their meetings. What would happen if Christians had that kind of enthusiasm? Nichiren followers say their religion does things for them. What does your faith do for you? Did you ever tell someone else about it? Should you?

CHURCH: Start Being

Thus says the Lord:
Oh you Christians, strength of my arm, voice of my mouth,
     compassion of my heart,
Step off your merry-go-round!
Break through your monotonous cycle!
   You who raise money to erect buildings,
    so you can expand your program,
and when you expand your program,
   you need more money to erect more buildings.
O when will you start *being* the church;
stop making the church a place to go to,
   and make it something to be;
stop building churches,
   and start being the Kingdom of God in the midst?
Stop making a basket case out of the Body of Christ!
Instead, make his Body active, virile and whole,
with hands outstretched in service,
   feet swift to do my bidding,
   eyes quick to see the world's need,
   ears open to hear your brother's cry for help.

—J. Elliott Corbett[1]

This is the way Dr. Corbett, a minister in Washington, D.C., translates the ancient message of Jeremiah into the language of today. Isn't it true that a church can get into the kind of "monotonous cycle" mentioned here, building programs and

[1] From *The Prophets on Main Street* (a paraphrase of a passage in Jeremiah) by J. Elliott Corbett. John Knox Press. Copyright © by M. E. Bratcher, 1965.

church buildings instead of being the Kingdom? Is a church a means or an end? What is the business of the church? What should its goals be today? Do these goals have to be the same as they were a hundred years ago—or the same as they may be in the year 20,000?

CHURCH: What the Church Must Do

"In the early 1930s Tillich predicted that the church would cease to function in modern secular society unless it could repossess the sacred by clothing it in symbolic and sacramental forms that communicate to contemporary man, unless it could demonstrate the intrinsic unity of the sacred and the secular, and unless it could maintain prophetic insight and power in pronouncing judgment on the claims for absolute authority made by secular institutions. These three tasks can be regarded as contemporary requirements for making known the meaning of the kingdom of God."[1]

Judged by these three standards, how is your church doing?

Do its symbols and sacraments have meaning for outsiders? Does it witness to a God who is Lord of both the holy and the commonplace, the church and the world? Does it have a divine word that transcends other claims for allegiance, making it clear that God alone has absolute authority over mankind?

Is this the message people hear—not only from the minister's sermons, but from the members' witness in their everyday talk and work?

CHURCH: Who Is Welcome?

Don Chappell is the son of Methodist missionaries and was raised in the Congo. He spent the summer of 1969 at Koinonia,

[1] *Theology: An Assessment of Current Trends,* The Lutheran Church in America (Fortress Press).

56

the experimental farm in Georgia where Clarence Jordan tried to express Christian love in new forms for our age. Don decided to contact the local Methodists in Americus, Georgia, where Koinonia is, and went to church. He took along some friends, including a Puerto Rican and a Negro.

The church's hospitality committee barred Don and his friends. Puzzled, Don talked with the pastor, who said he ought to get a haircut (his hair was about two inches longer than a GI's) and a decent shirt (Don was wearing a Congolese dress shirt). Don Chappell went back to Koinonia, had his hair cut, and changed to an American shirt and tie. Then he went back to talk to the pastor again. This time the minister told him he would not be welcome until he got rid of his non-white friends. He added that he personally regretted the church's policy, but the people did not want people with dark skins in their church, and he was not planning to buck the policy.

Don was upset. He had thought Christians in America wanted black people and brown people to come to Christ. The Americus people said they *do*, but not in their church.

Should churches follow the color bars of the society around them? Probably few churches today physically bar non-whites; do most of them welcome everyone? What would your church do if an alcoholic came to the next service? What sort of reception would there be for a man just out of jail? Would your garbage collector feel welcome in your church? Who should be welcome? Who should not be?

THE CHURCH AND ITS MINISTERS: Do We Support Them?

The average church is highly conscious of its financial support of its minister—but do most churches really *support* their clergy? This question must be asked in the light of a November 1969 release of the National Council of Churches researched by Edgar W. Mills and Janet F. Morse.

The report emphasizes not averages but medians. Close to but not quite the same as an average, a median is that point in a list where there are as many items above as below. The report reveals that the median income of the full-time Protestant minister in the United States in 1968 was $8037. This means that as many ministers had less than that income as had more. (One sixth of America's full-time pastors received less than $6000.) This amount in each case includes an estimate of $1913 for housing and utilities and gifts; in other words, the median pastor's actual salary is $6124. Furthermore, the study shows that 78 percent of the clergy incur a net *loss* of $1018 for use of auto, attending denominational meetings, etc., so the usable cash income is barely more than $5000.

This is less than the income of a city worker with very low living standards in a family of four. The median income of an accountant is $9367; a personnel director, $13,215; an attorney, $15,283; a chemist with equivalent education to the average minister, $16,000.

With constantly rising prices, no wonder a fourth of America's ministers, in the last five years, have had to go further into debt; 26 percent say the need for money is a serious problem; twice as many ministers' wives now have jobs as in 1963; 71 percent of the clergy feel their salaries are too low; so many are leaving the ministry—although the National Council of Churches found that only 10 percent of those surveyed (a random sampling of thousands of clergymen) plan to go into some other kind of work.

Do we really *support* our ministers? St. Paul told Timothy, "The laborer is worthy of his reward" (I Timothy 5:18). Apparently most of us don't believe in very big rewards for our spiritual leaders.

Does your church care? Forty-five percent of America's ministers do not receive an annual review of their compensation. They should. Every church should have a committee to talk with its pastor about his salary, review current living costs and the pastor's needs (What shape is his car in? Does he have children ready to go to college?), and see that he does not have to live in shame and destitution.

A fine guidebook for such a committee has been prepared by the Ministers Life and Casualty Union, Minneapolis, Minnesota, which financed the National Council's study. Your own denomination is also eager to help see that your church has all the resources available to provide your minister with an adequate income.

CHURCH AND MISSION: What Are We Doing?

"One local church, in a policy-planning session, went through lengthy hours of study and discussion and finally reached the climactic night of decision. The final discussion was long, and there was a notable lack of consensus. Unbelievable as it may sound, this motion was finally placed upon the books: 'I move that we continue to do what we have always done, whatever that is.' "[1]

How many church members are better informed than those who agreed to that motion? Do the members of your church have a clear idea of what your church is doing, what it is trying to accomplish, and why? If they don't, why don't they? Exactly what is the church trying to do?

CHURCH FOR TODAY: What Is a Minister?

Lloyd John Ogilvie is the pastor of a dynamic church in Bethlehem, Pennsylvania. But he insists that he is not the minister. In fact, the church has rewritten its constitution to make every member a minister. In the New Testament, of course, "minister" means simply "servant." Catholics know that, officially, their pope is "servant of the servants of God." Members of Bethlehem's First Presbyterian Church know that

[1] *Ventures in Mission* by Paul O. Madsen (Friendship Press).

the job of their pastors is to encourage and enable them, the minister-members, to do the real work of the church: taking the life and joy of Christ into their jobs, their neighborhoods, their social relationships.

Dr. Ogilvie once told of a member who phoned him to say, "I have a free evening tonight. Anything I can do for you?" The pastor gave him the name and address of a family that needed the kind of help a committed Christian can give. The minister-member followed through for months until that whole family was amazingly helped by this layman's witness.

Are you a minister?

CIGARETTES AND HUMOR

Now that there is little question how dangerous cigarette smoking is, many who were once smokers smoke no longer. But many remain unconvinced—in spite of the many studies that show the intimate relationship, statistically, between cigarettes and lung cancer, heart disease, emphysema, and many other diseases.

Dr. Wayman Spence uses humor to jar smokers. One of his inventions, which he has given to many people, is a lung ashtray. Above the ashtray is a plastic model of a pair of human lungs. One lung is closed; the other is open to the cigarette smoke from the ashtray. The open lung becomes stained with tobacco tar from the smoke, reminding smokers what the stuff is doing to their own lungs.

Dr. Spence has also coined a number of smoking slogans which are included in his *Ban the Butt Button Book*. Among them:

SMOKING MAKES YOU REAL GONE—
    ABOUT 8 YEARS SOONER.
TO KILL A MOCKINGBIRD, BLOW SMOKE ON IT.
ORPHAN ANNIE'S PARENTS SMOKED.
SMOKE TODAY—GONE TOMORROW.

THE FAMILY THAT SMOKES TOGETHER CHOKES TOGETHER. DYING FOR A SMOKE?

Sometimes satire reaches people when facts don't.

CIGARETTES AND MORALITY

A recent survey commissioned by the United States Public Health Service shows that an increasing proportion of cigarette smokers believe the practice is morally wrong. In 1964, 16 percent of the male smokers questioned and 13 percent of the women smokers said they thought smoking was wrong. In 1969, 45 percent of the men and 47 percent of the women said they thought it was wrong.

Evidently, even smokers who do not want to give up the habit recognize the harmful effect on the body which is statistically evident from scientific research. But how sad it is to violate one's conscience by deliberately continuing to do what one knows is wrong.

Is there any longer any defense for coffin nails?

See also COURTESY AND TOBACCO, PERSISTENCE AND SUCCESS

CITIES AND SUBURBS

> Night has fallen on the city?
> Courage, Brother—do not fear.
> Let us bear the cross together
> To suburbia's frontier.[1]

Faced by decaying communities, members moving away, and unresponsive foreign-born people moving in, many churches have deserted the cities for the suburbs. Ken Anderson's ironic lines are not the last word, however. The suburban churches are taking a new look at themselves, asking what their role

[1] Ken Anderson in *Stains on Glass Windows* (Word Books).

and purpose are, and whether a church has a right to settle down country-club style among the comforts of the wealthiest areas in the world's wealthiest country.

Some churches are moving back into the cities. Others are yoking together with inner-city churches, the one helping financially while the other helps with the challenges of the exciting new needs and problems of today's downtown.

What are churches for? How comfortable does a church have a right to be? In these days when many parts of the world are closed to foreign missions, where is there a greater need for the Christian message than in the crowded, chaotic, seemingly near-hopeless areas at the center of our cities?

CIVILIZATION THAT IS CHRISTIAN: Are We Afraid to Try?

"The truth is," writes Alan Paton in his great novel *Cry, the Beloved Country,* "that our Christian civilization is riddled through and through with dilemma. We believe that God endows men with diverse gifts, and that human life depends for its fulness on their employment and enjoyment, but we are afraid to explore this belief too deeply.

"We believe in help for the underdog, but we want him to stay under. . . . The truth is that our civilization is not Christian, it is a tragic compound of great ideal and fearful practice, of high assurance and desperate anxiety, of loving charity and fearful clutching of possessions."

Alan Paton wrote primarily of his own civilization in South Africa. Does what he says apply to us? Are we, too, afraid to explore what we believe very deeply? Most of us want to help the city beggar, the uneducated migrant child, the Indian on his desolate reservation, and the black person in his ghetto. At the same time, are we afraid to help too much? Do we secretly hope the underdog stays under?

There is a parable about a man who buried his talent because he was afraid. Are we willing to face our fears, to let the love of Christ replace them with courageous acts of justice? Is God waiting for us to form a truly Christian civilization? Are we willing to be Christian through and through?

COMMANDMENTS AND COURTROOMS

Four men held up a grocery store in Louisville, Kentucky, and in the process shot and killed two policemen. When the men were brought to trial, their lawyer noticed a copy of the Ten Commandments on the wall near the jury box.

"Judge Hayes," said the attorney, "that framed reproduction of the Commandments is detrimental to this trial. I request that it be removed lest it adversely influence this jury."

The judge said he did not believe the document would prejudice the trial and refused to have the Decalogue removed from the courtroom. Some people present observed that among the Commandments were these: "Thou shalt not steal"; "Thou shalt not kill."

The Commandments remained in the courtroom.

Some years ago, Dr. Elton Trueblood commented that one thing Catholics, Protestants, and Jews hold in common is the Ten Commandments, and suggested that they are one thing all Americans should be able to agree upon. Without these basic principles of respect for God and man, what is left? We suggest that if anyone is going to construct a new morality, here is the place to begin.

It is true that the ancient Commandments have sometimes been misinterpreted to defend slavery and various other sins against humanity. We suggest that everyone take a new look at these ten principles, which at the very least represent the distilled wisdom of the three great faiths of man—and to Christians and Jews are words from God which we must not ignore. Properly understood, here are the principles of reverence for God, respect for life, honor among men.

How are the Ten Commandments to be interpreted? Do they justify slavery? Do they justify a corporation or a nation in taking someone else's property and then invoking the same Commandments against someone who tries to get it back?

What did Jesus say about the ancient laws of God? (See Matthew 5–7.) What is the basis of Christian morality?

See also MORALITY.

COMMITMENT AND DIRECTION

Reviewing a book about a former First Lady of the United States, Marylin Bender wrote in the New York *Times Book Review:* ". . . the former First Lady emerges as a lonely, uncommitted and misdirected woman of heroic strengths that she seems only able to summon when facing disaster. In tranquil times, she fritters away her intelligence and numerous talents."

How tragic—to let exceptional gifts dribble away, and to be uncommitted in an age when commitment and dedication are so important and necessary. But rather than waste our time criticizing someone whose problems and temptations we cannot know, let us ask:

Is this one reason why disasters are permitted—to summon us to heights we would not otherwise know we could reach? What gifts and talents do we fritter away? To what or whom are we really committed?

COMMUNES AND PRIVATE PROPERTY

One of the interesting new developments of this generation is the fast-spreading commune—the multifamily home, in which a number of people live together like one big family. A close-knit community in which everything is shared, it is appearing in various parts of the world and may be a widespread practice in the future. Something quite similar appears to have characterized the early Christian community:

64

"And all that believed were together, and had all things common; and sold their possessions and goods, and parted them to all men, as every man had need" (Acts 2:45).

Sociologists have pointed out that this age in America is one of the first to destroy children's contact with the older generation. In past ages the family often lived on a farm, usually in a large house, with grandparents and sometimes other relatives under the same roof. A child learned not only from his own parents but from various other adults with whom he had a continuing close contact. Today the average American house has no room for relatives, the grandparents are in Florida or a nursing home, and the child's close contacts with adults are limited largely to his parents. Perhaps the rise of the commune will restore the richer relationships of earlier generations.

On the other hand, many of us take pride in our personal possessions. The right of private property may not be an article of faith with us, but we share the point of view of Rachel Hartnett, who wrote:

No Commune

No commune will ever interest me.
I want to own, alone,
MY plot of land, MY little house,
Each timber, pane and stone.

And when in time it needs repairs
I'll never be aloof,
I'll gladly fix the troubles in
MY floor, MY walls, MY roof.

I'll even sing a little song
(In voice not quite high-class)
When toiling, sweating, digging up
MY darned old devil grass.[1]

What is the basis of private property? How absolute were property rights in Biblical times? (See Leviticus 19:9–18, 23–25.

[1] Printed in *Arizona Highways*, February 1970. Used by permission.

What does this tell us about ancient property rights? About the rights of others to our property?) What is the appeal of personal possessions? What are the advantages of sharing things with others? Do sharing and private property rights have to be opposed to each other?

COMPASSION: Older than We Thought?

"Forty thousand years ago in the bleak uplands of southwestern Asia, a man, a Neanderthal man . . . existed with a fearful body handicap in that ice-age world. He had lost an arm. But still he lived and was cared for. Somebody, some group of human things, in a hard, violent and stony world, loved this maimed creature enough to cherish him."[1]

Ancient man is often depicted as low-browed, hairy, bestial, brutal. This is incorrect. Scientists are now carefully correcting the pictures and statues of hairy "apemen" to show how similar men of the past were to men today. The man who lost an arm forty thousand years ago, the evidence shows, was not eaten, not abandoned, but was shown care and compassion by other members of his group.

Ancient man filled his caves with remarkable carvings and paintings—and worship, and love. Concern for others is not something invented in the twentieth century. It is apparently as old as humanity—or as life itself, for nature is full of examples of the care and affection of birds, animals, fish, and even whales, for one another.

Lust and cruelty are often identified with manhood. What is manly about them? What is more human, or divine, than concern and compassion and caring?

CONCERN: Does Anybody Care?

America's Office of Economic Opportunity concerns itself with people like Miss Doris Anderson. Late in 1969, for the

[1] Loren Eiseley in *The Firmament of Time* (Atheneum), pp. 144–45.

first time in her life, she fell behind in her rent, and when her landlord threatened to evict her she appealed for help to the Baltimore Social Service. After the fashion of bureaucracies, the welfare worker whom she asked for help sent her to another worker, who sent her back to the first one, who by then was too busy (his receptionist said) to see her. Since it was now late in the day and Miss Anderson did not want to be evicted from her apartment, she tried to find the welfare worker herself.

Guards appeared and called the police. Miss Anderson heard them asking what to charge her with. Denied a lawyer or contact with anyone, she was grilled by two elderly doctors and put in a hospital for the insane, where she was set to scrubbing floors. Perhaps she would still be there if the OEO had not discovered her disappearance, investigated, proved there was no reason for her incarceration, and got her released.

Nicholas von Hoffman, who told of Miss Anderson's experience in the Washington *Post* for January 26, 1970, comments: "The worst thing about what happened to Miss Anderson is its accidental aspect. Nobody was out to get her; there's no evidence showing it was racial malice [she is black] or a special grudge. She might have been a mother with a sick child or an old person whose children wanted to get rid of her. The whole business was so casual, so indifferent—the doctor couldn't remember her name. Aw, don't bother with her, arrest her, she's a nut, put her away."

Perhaps Doris Anderson was one of the casualties of the population explosion. When there are so many people making demands on you all day that you weary of them, the easiest thing to do with a "problem" individual is to get the person out of sight—especially if he or she is poor or non-white. Sometimes I dream that I am trapped among giant machines and there is no way out. In some ways our whole society is trapped by giant machines and corporations and organizations. Somewhere a board of directors fires a manager and hires another one to get more profits for a group of people somewhere else who are the stockholders. The manager has

67

been employed to make those profits, so he is on the spot to cut every corner and make every dollar possible. So we end with advertising men lying about a product they are hired to sell, the manufacturer raising the price and cheapening the contents to make more money, and an endless chain of individuals who finally sell the man in the store a fake. All these people are simply doing a job, trying to make a living, cogs in giant wheels that grind out inflation, danger, and sometimes death to unsuspecting victims. No one means any harm; no one person is responsible, but the dental product doesn't prevent decay, the food doesn't nourish, the new car may be a death trap.

Of course the above is not true of all products. Some products are excellent—and some were once excellent but are now increasingly worse because someone somewhere is trying to make more money faster at someone else's expense.

What can Christians do about our mechanized, impersonal society? Can one person alone do much? Can he do something? Does he have a right—or a responsibility—to band together with others to work for fair business practices, honest advertising, responsibility in public institutions? Is this something the government should be involved in? Business? The churches?

Who is to see that the next Miss Anderson gets back out of that prison or asylum?

CONCERN: Who Are You?

"I can't help wondering: Who are you? I wonder what are your dreams, the things that make you laugh, the people you love, the deep loyalties which stir you to act, the basic dictates of your conscience, and the vision of truth which cuts through your life."[1]

Well? How do you get to know what a person is really like without knowing some of these things? What were the

[1] Malcolm Boyd in *As I Live and Breathe.*

deepest loyalties and concerns of Jesus Christ? What did He feel about hungry people, defrauded widows, ordinary people who were oppressed and misled? Why are we on earth? What can we do to make the journey of life more worthwhile? What do we care about most of all?

CONFESSION OF SIN: The New Catholicism

Confession before Mass, for Catholics, used to be the subject of a number of jokes among Protestants, some of whom felt that confession was a mechanical ritual. Now many Catholics seem to agree, at least in part.

In Minneapolis, Minnesota, five Roman Catholic churches have begun to substitute "communal penance" services for the old-style confession. The services emphasize Scripture reading, public examination of conscience, prayer, hymns, and a sermon. During the service each person makes a brief personal confession to a priest. *Religious News Service* quotes Father Joseph Baglio as saying that parishioners are being encouraged "to move away from the routine, grocery-list type of confession" to plans for making their future behavior more Christian. Father Eugene J. Roden says the old form of confession became too routine with too little appreciation of the value of sorrow for sin.

As Catholics move away from the faults in their way of worship, Protestants may well learn again the importance of sincere confession of sin to God and others. Alcoholics Anonymous have built a very impressive program for overcoming alcoholism in twelve steps, one of them confession "to God and one other person."

What is the value in confessing sins? Are there religious practices in our lives that have become too routine? How can we keep our spiritual life fresh and meaningful?

CONFLICTS: Solution by Personal Encounter

In 1949, twenty years before President Nixon recommended increased contact and discussion with Red China, Dr. John A. Mackay advocated such encounter. His suggestion brought instant charges from many people that he (one of America's and Christianity's most respected missionaries and Christian leaders) was a Communist or a Communist-sympathizer.

"However," he wrote in the January 2, 1970, issue of *Christianity Today,* "my position has remained unchanged. In the solution of issues that involve conflict or misunderstanding between persons or between nations, whoever they be, there is a timeless imperative. There can be no substitute for quiet, frank, face-to-face encounter. The incarnational approach applies to all human relationships."

When there is conflict between individuals, should we accept this as final or try to resolve it? How? Is there any substitute for person-to-person discussion in a sincere attempt to locate the problem and restore any broken relationship? If this works on an individual basis, why not nation-to-nation?

For reference: Isaiah 32:17; I Thessalonians 5:13; Matthew 5:23-24.

CONFORMITY OR INDIVIDUALISM? Daring to Be Different

"I think of the pressures there are in present-day society to get people, young people especially, to consent to and acquiesce in sub-Christian standards of culture: 'Conform, or be left out!'— which is secularism's dreary reversal of the ancient word, 'Be not conformed to this world, but be transformed by the renewing of your mind.' I think of one of the greatest and most urgent of international problems, the question of the proliferation of nuclear weapons and the dangers of nuclear tests. Christians may take one side or another quite sincerely. There are diversities of judgment here. But at least we are bound to say this, that if any Christian, after deep, long searching of his soul and endeavouring to find the mind of Christ, should feel moved to speak out for abolition of such tests, and then encounters the contemptuous retort that he is a poor dupe, a misguided meddler, an unconscious victim of alien subtle propaganda—this at any rate is a libel and a lie."[1]

How does a Christian decide when to go along with the crowd and when to protest? . . . Do we ever feel that someone is a "misguided dupe"?

See also PROTESTS.

COUNSELING DRAFTEES: A Chaplain's View

By the look of things early in 1970, the war in Vietnam will be a problem for young people for a number of years. The Reverend Galen Meyer addresses himself in the magazine *The Young Calvinist* for February, 1970, to a question a young man may ask: "Should I participate or not?"

Since Meyer has served as a chaplain (Christian Reformed) in Vietnam, what he says has the merit of firsthand knowledge of the subject.

In making a decision, the Reverend Mr. Meyer points out, there are two important guidelines or principles from Scripture to take into consideration. One is this: As a general rule, the government must be obeyed (Romans 13:1–2). But there is another very important principle: If the government requires us to do anything we believe is an outrage against our Christian duty, "We must obey God, not men" (Acts 5:29).

"God gave you a head with which to think and a heart with which to feel," writes Meyer. "He expects you to use both. . . ." Meyer suggests studying, reading, talking with people, finding out as much as possible about the Vietnam War. Then the decision must be made—either to accept the

[1] James S. Stewart, *The Wind of the Spirit* (Abingdon Press and Hodder and Stoughton, Ltd.). Used by permission.

draft as a soldier, go as a medic, or become an objector. Two of the easier roads, given the latter choice, would be to take refuge in a foreign country or to register as a conscientious objector to all wars. One of the hardest routes is selective conscientious objection—deciding that, while you are not a pacifist, you cannot conscientiously fight in this particular war in Vietnam. "Our government will not recognize your declaration . . . ," says Meyer. "You might face ridicule, court costs, and a prison term of one or more years. These are the hard facts.

"The only choice you have is to accept these hard facts as the 'cost of discipleship,' the bill you estimated worth paying when you first decided to follow the Galilean."

Whatever you decide, you will find many people in disagreement. "Many people will consider your decision wrong, but that is not important. What is important is that you are honestly convinced the decision you made is right."

Do you agree with the two central guidelines the Reverend Chaplain Meyer gives? Can a young person expect your sympathy and support even though he comes to a different conclusion than you do about participating in the war? Does a Christian ever have the right to disobey his government? Does a Christian ever have the right to do what he knows is wrong even though his government commands it? Do we have a right to say the Nazis or Communists are wrong in obeying their governments if we lack the courage, when necessary, to put God ahead of government?

See also WAR, YOUNG PEOPLE AND WAR.

COURTESY AND TOBACCO

Early in 1970, Warren E. Burger sent a letter to the head of the Federal Aviation Administration, suggesting a proposal about smoking on airplanes. In his letter Mr. Burger told of a flight he had taken from Washington to Minneapolis during which so many people were smoking that even the stewardesses had reddened eyes. He protested to the airline's president, but said he was "not even accorded the courtesy of an answer" to his letter. The 1970 letter, however, got an answer. FAA Administrator John Shaffer promised to do something. One reason the second letter received a reply may be that Mr. Burger is now the Chief Justice of the United States Supreme Court.

Smoking on airplanes, said the *Wall Street Journal's* Albert R. Karr in his report of the Burger incidents on January 29, 1970, may not only injure the tempers and health of those subjected to the smokers' exhalation, but may create fire hazards, cause accidents, and even gum up the airplane's instruments. A contributing factor in the collison between one airliner and a private plane may have been a fire in the cockpit, caused by a live cigarette in an ashtray. If the crew had not been distracted by the fire, they might have been able to avoid the collision in which eighty-two people lost their lives.

Are nonsmokers more courteous than smokers? Now that we know how much harm cigarettes may cause, is there any good reason they should be advertised so heavily?

See also CIGARETTES AND HUMOR, PERSISTENCE AND SUCCESS.

CRIME AND JUSTICE: Is Legal Punishment Just?[1]

"Punishment is in part an attitude, a philosophy. It is the deliberate infliction of pain in addition to or in lieu of penalty. It is the prolonged and excessive infliction of penalty, or penalty out of all proportion to the offense. Detention in prison was supposed to be a mollification of pain infliction, but it is often more cruel and destructive than beating. What is gained for anybody when a man who has forged a check for sixty dollars

[1] The following excerpt is from *The Crime of Punishment* by Karl Menninger. Copyright © 1966, 1968 by Karl Menninger, M.D. All Rights Reserved. Reprinted by permission of The Viking Press, Inc.

is sentenced to the penitentiary for *thirty years* (at public expense, of course)? I saw such a case in 1967. The judge's rationalization was that the man had offended in this way *twice before*(!) and had served shorter sentences without reforming.

"This is not penalization. This is not correction. This is not public protection. (Is any check forger so dangerous as to require such expensive precautions?) This is not reformation. It is sadistic persecution of the helpless at public expense, justified by the 'punishment' principle.

"When a seventy-seven-year-old woman driving her car in heavy traffic struck and killed an eight-year-old child, everyone concerned, including the parents of the child, the judge, and the woman herself, agreed that she should renounce driving forever; this was her penalty. No 'punishment' was imposed.

"If a burglar takes my property, I would like to have it returned or paid for by him, if possible, and the state ought to be reimbursed for its costs, too. This could be forcibly required to come from the burglar. This would be equitable; it would be just and it would not be 'punitive.' Just *what* the penalties should be in the case of many offenses is a big question, I realize, but it could be answered if all the public vengeance and lust for seeing people hurt by punishment could be ignored."

The Prophet Micah asked, "And what doth the Lord require of thee, but to do justly . . . ?" (*Micah 6:8*).

Dr. Menninger, founder with his father of the renowned Menninger Clinic, makes a convincing case in his book *The Crime of Punishment* for the thesis that our usual form of punishment for crime is itself a crime. The way we usually treat those convicted of wrongdoing, he argues, is often so partial, so slow, so unjust—with the worst kind of criminals getting relatively light or no sentences while individuals only once convicted of some very slight misdemeanor may receive cruel and unusual punishment—that it is itself a crime. To expose youthful first offenders—and, more often, those arrested on someone's suspicion and later proved innocent—to the mental and physical corruption of hardened criminals and of guards in league with gangsters, is a crime against our whole society.

The world-famous German theologian Karl Barth took a lifelong interest in prisons; when he visited the United States the last time before his death, he made a special point of visiting various prisons here, and he found the conditions in some of them shocking.

How many Christians know what the inside of a prison is like? Should we? What did Jesus have to say about prisons? How could a prayerful reading of Matthew 25:31–46 help things?

See also JUSTICE.

CRIME AND THE POOR: Is There a Solution?

In every society there are basically two classes, the privileged and the underprivileged. The Puerto Ricans in New York, the blacks in Mississippi, the Mexican-Americans in the Southwest generally have these characteristics: inadequate diet, crowded housing, vitamin deficiencies, venereal and other diseases. Incredibly large numbers are crowded into one or two rooms. A youngster from an eastern city said, "The only time in my life I had a whole bed to myself was when I went to camp." Under such conditions, children learn about sex early.

Two Mexican-American minors were charged with incest late in 1969 in California's Superior Court. Judge Gerald S. Chargin said to the alleged offender, according to a transcript of the court proceedings: "You are lower than an animal. . . . You are no particular good to anybody. We ought to send you out of the country—send you back to Mexico. You belong in prison for the rest of your life for doing things of this kind. You ought to commit suicide. . . . Maybe Hitler was right. The animals in our society ought to be destroyed because they have no right to live among human beings."

Judge Chargin's solution to the problem of crime among the underprivileged is apparently to "destroy" them. *If the majority of people a child meets have such an attitude toward him, how much self-esteem can he retain? Is it any wonder that the suicide rate among young blacks and Indians is many times the national average, or that crime statistics are high?*

Is there a solution? Several Presidential commissions have investigated the problem of American crime and juvenile delinquency. All of them have reached the conclusion that crime and social conditions are inextricably bound together, and that we can make no real progress against crime unless we also war against poverty, slums, and all the other things that create the conditions of crime. Are these learned men correct?

Many churches are investing in better housing and in helping to find jobs for the poor.

Which is better, this procedure, or consigning those convicted (or charged with an offense) to destruction?

CRIME AND PUNISHMENT—or Justice?

"The very word *justice* irritates scientists," says the noted psychiatrist Karl Menninger in his excellent book *The Crime of Punishment*. He points out that when a surgeon sees a cancer he simply tries to remove it without expecting to be asked whether his operation is "just" or not.

Scientists who study human behavior, Dr. Menninger adds, consider it equally absurd to bring in the abstract concept of justice when trying to treat a woman who cannot resist the impulse to shoplift, or a man who feels an uncontrollable urge to assault someone. "This sort of behavior has to be controlled; it has to be discouraged; it has to be stopped. This (to the scientist) is a matter of public safety and amicable coexistence, not of justice."

If a person cannot stop stealing or drinking, is this a matter for punishment by locking him or her away in degradation and sometimes perversion and physical danger—or for seeking a cure? And even if the person is locked away, does this serve justice or prevention? Dr. Menninger argues persuasively that this is not an area where the legal concept of justice belongs, but rather medical diagnosis and cure. Is it just to lock up "criminals" who happen to be caught (and many are either not caught, or buy their way out of conviction or punishment) among hardened criminals, psychopaths, and sexual perverts? Under our present system crime is increasing every year. Should we consider amending the system?

CRIME IN GOVERNMENT: Too Strong to Root Out?

" 'Is he okay?' Those three words are practically a password among politicians and policemen in New Jersey. You hear that question about a purchasing agent in a Jersey City hospital, about an assistant prosecutor in Essex County, about an important state senator in Trenton. 'Is he okay?'

"An 'okay' guy is one who isn't going to cause trouble, a 'reasonable' man who knows something is going on but is either in on it or has learned that it's wiser to look the other way and keep his mouth shut.

"Something has been going on in Jersey for a long time— every once in a while someone who isn't okay talks about it. The latest to speak out is Frederick B. Lacey, the United States Attorney for New Jersey, who has said: 'Organized crime, in the vernacular, is taking us over. For a few rotten dollars mobsters have been able to corrupt officials in various governments. Organized crime will not even go into a community unless and until it has bought protection against raids and arrests.'

"Strong words. But other prosecutors have used the same kind of words in the past, and after they spoke out they were thrown out."[1]

[1] Richard Reeves, "Another Crime Buster Tries to Break the Mafia in New Jersey," © 1970 by The New York Times Company. Reprinted by permission.

Reporter Reeves's shocking indictment of crime embedded in government includes the statement that New Jersey crime is nonpartisan: Both Republicans and Democrats, he says, cooperate with gangsters against the people.

Reeves lists occasion after occasion when information about crime was ignored by state and county officials, when investigators were removed from office because the truth hurt someone too high in politics.

New Jersey is not the only state, we suspect, where crime and government form an incredible partnership. But isn't it sickening that such things can happen in a country that likes to offer moral leadership to the world?

Our coins proclaim, "In God We Trust." Do we—in hard fact? In the actualities of political life? Can we expect young people to reverence law and order if the law and order are controlled by thugs and gangsters?

In one New Jersey town the church people and their ministers got together and put a crimp in the criminal stranglehold on their community. That involved hard, painstaking, dangerous work. Should this be a pattern for Christian action elsewhere— or should Christians stick to "religion" only?

CRITICISM: Can It Do Any Good?

Robert B. Downs is the author of an interesting book about books. Published in March, 1970, under the title *Books That Changed America,* it treats of the influence of such books as *Uncle Tom's Cabin,* which helped destroy American slavery; *The Jungle,* which led to important reforms in the meat-packing industry; and Rachel Carson's *Silent Spring,* which warned of the dangers of pesticides a decade before anyone in a position to protect the public took that farsighted scientist seriously. A review of the book in *Publishers' Weekly* comments: "Downs doesn't say it, but Americans seem to have been affected most by the books that criticized them most severely."[1]

[1] February 2, 1970, p. 83.

Few of us feel happy when we are criticized. Yet criticism itself need not have the negative connotations often associated with it. The word comes from a Greek word meaning separation, discrimination, judgment. The critics weigh the merits of a book or dramatic production, and many of us depend upon them for their estimates of the many works we do not have time to read or see.

Love may cover a multitude of sins, but love may have to speak. St. Paul extolled the value of "speaking the truth in love" (Ephesians 4:15). Could a person who loved his country let it slide downhill without doing or saying anything to stop the decline? Were you ever helped by truthful criticism? Is all criticism worthwhile?

DAILY LIFE AND OUR FAITH: Eternal Principles or Specific Application?

The churches of my denomination send representatives to area meetings, called presbyteries, at which we discuss matters of common interest. At one such meeting there was a discussion of the need many of us felt for a state income tax. This, we believed, was the fairest way for the state to fulfill its moral responsibility toward the poor, the retarded, the disadvantaged, the mentally ill, etc. There was a proposal that we go on record favoring such a tax.

One minister vehemently opposed this. "The church," he said, "must proclaim the great moral principles frankly and fully. But it must never recommend specific political measures."

The problem of some of us is: How do you do that? How can you say anything very effective or meaningful about an issue if you never get down to brass tacks and name names?

Granted, it would not be very wise for a preacher to tell people who he thinks they should vote for in the next election. But if he seriously thinks that gambling, for example, is harmful to a community, would he not do well to say so, and to urge his people to vote against legislation that would legalize gambling?

Dietrich Bonhoeffer, this century's German martyr, felt strongly about this. He insisted, says W. A. Visser 't Hooft in *The Steps of Bonhoeffer,* "that the church does not exist in order to proclaim eternal truths or principles, but in order to tell men what God's message is here and now in the most concrete way." Bonhoeffer, realizing the monstrosity of Nazism's attempts to subvert the Christian message, exterminate the Jewish people, and enslave the free countries, actively opposed his own government's policies and was executed as an enemy of the state.

Does the Bible give us eternal principles or specific examples of God's will? It is *humans* who read into the eighth Commandment "the right of private property"; *God* says, "Thou shalt not steal." When Jesus preached, he talked about specifics: healing blind people, telling good news to the poor, helping a man who had been beaten by robbers, giving cold water to a thirsty man. He called certain people hypocrites and he was not at all vague about the reason: "You eat up the property of widows, while you say long prayers" (Matthew 23:14 NEB).

Are principles of much value unless we practice them in everyday life? About specific issues on which Christians take sides, some say we don't know enough to take a position. Do we ever know enough about anything to be absolutely sure what to do? Should this keep us from ever doing anything?

See also EVERYDAY CHRISTIANITY, FAITH AND EVERYDAY WORK.

DEATH AND RESURRECTION, 1970–1980

"If I had to preach an Easter sermon," a friend told me, "I don't know what I'd say. Years ago it would have been no problem, but now I'm not so sure."

I think I know what he meant. Some of the old sermons and symbols don't hold up very well in this age of atomic power and space travel. Yet this new age makes some things clearer than ever. For one thing, *death isn't final.*

Many of us will never get over the traumatic experience of Dallas, November 22, 1963. A President was shot. And then the great King, who held so much promise for keeping our racially torn nation united, was assassinated, and then a senator who might have become a second President Kennedy. All gone, erased by bullets in the hands of people who thought bullets were the last word.

They aren't. When John Kennedy went down, surely thousands of men and women and young people vowed to give their lives, as he had given his, to make the America of their dreams and pledges a reality. Killing King didn't kill the hopes of millions of black and white Americans of achieving liberty and justice for all. Assassinating the Senator, far from ending his concern for justice, for peace, for righting the wrongs done to red and brown as well as black minorities, multiplied it.

When I was younger I used to think that talk of someone's spirit living on in other people's lives was so much sentimentality. Now I know it is real. We have all seen it in recent years, whether we think of the Kennedys or of someone like Che Guevara—killed by assassins, but very much alive in the thoughts and deeds of many young people.

Consider Dietrich Bonhoeffer—a young German theologian of tremendous promise, snugly hidden away at New York's Union Theological Seminary when Hitler's Nazis started their mad campaign against humanity. He could have made powerful contributions to our age if he had stayed alive and well at Union, but he saw his country going up in flames and he returned home to fight them. When the Nazis hanged him for conspiring to kill Hitler, Bonhoeffer was only thirty-nine. But his influence is far greater in this troubled time of questionable allegiances and uncertainties than if he had played it safe.

Bonhoeffer had time to write few books. One of them, *The Cost of Discipleship,* is very influential today because the author lived what he wrote, and did not shrink from paying the cost. It is his life as much as his words that helps us, too, to live our faith in a complex world.

Jesus said it two millenniums ago: "Except a corn of wheat fall into the ground and die, it abideth alone: but if it die, it bringeth forth much fruit" (John 12:24).

See also IMMORTALITY, RESURRECTION.

DEFENSE AND PEACE

Most Americans are aware that most of their tax money is spent on what we sometimes call "the defense effort." And most are not unwilling to "keep America strong," in spite of the immense burden on the citizens, if this will truly help keep the peace.

Catholic Cardinal John Krol is not sure that all those armaments produce peace. At a World Day of Peace gathering of his church in Philadelphia early in 1970 he said that peace "cannot be built by violence," according to the *National Register* of January 18, 1970, and urged that the amount of money this nation spends for arms be reduced sharply. He spoke of the dangerous game of brinkmanship sometimes played—when a country bluffs its way clear to the edge of the precipice of total war, hoping the other side will cry for peace first. (Doesn't it remind you of the game of "chicken," sometimes played by teen-agers, who wait to see who will be first to grab the uncontrolled steering wheel of a speeding car?) He said, "We must reverse and redirect our efforts for the attainment of peace. We must do so with the same commitment of men and resources that we have poured into the preparation and prosecution of wars."

Cardinal Krol pointed out that the world spent nearly $200 billion for armaments in 1969, and that if it increases at that rate, the amount will be *$4 trillion* ($4 million multiplied by a thousand times a thousand!) before 1980. He asked whether our American military budget, "which seems to escalate by a self-generating mechanism, is not itself a threat to our national security and destiny, as well as a monstrous expense to humanity." He added, "It is encouraging to see the increasing number of legislators who no longer respond to the panic button that national security is being endangered."

We assume that spending billions to make war will bring peace. Yet in the past, every time nations have built up their arms in "defense," they have ended in war. *Is it time for a new approach? Are Cardinal Krol, and all those who question the build-up of new devices to kill people, correct? Is it true, as Jesus warned, that "all who take the sword will perish by the sword" (Matthew 26:52)? Do we really believe that "Blessed are the peacemakers"?*

A banner in a city church contained the words "peace" and "love." "What is that rag doing in our church?" spluttered an irate church member to the pastor, threatening to withhold his money. How many times do the words "peace" and "love" occur in the New Testament? It might be a worthwhile exercise to get a dictionary, index, or concordance of the Bible and check some of these references, noting what God has to say about love and peace.

See also PEACE, WAR, YOUNG PEOPLE AND WAR.

DEHUMANIZATION

Early in 1970 a United States Army lieutenant went on trial for the premeditated murder of a Vietnamese prisoner. Army documents allege that Lieutenant James Duffy conspired with Sergeant John Lanasa to commit the murder, and that at the time Lanasa said, "I always wanted to shoot a gook between the eyes."[1]

According to reports, many GIs in Vietnam customarily refer to citizens of the country as "gooks," "dinks," and "slants." Verbal contempt becomes the prelude to torture and murder. So warfare often proceeds: In World War I, Americans called the Germans "Huns" and accused them of unspeakable atroci-

[1] The New York *Times,* February 8, 1970.

ties; and in World War II "Nazis" and "Japs" were associated with unbelievable acts of inhumanity. While many Nazi acts were indeed inhuman, is this an excuse for judging every citizen of a nation with whom we are at war as bestial and below contempt?

Overpopulation and mechanization are degrading enough without our consciously accelerating the dehumanization of fellow humans. Is this what Jesus was warning against when he said, "Anyone who nurses anger against his brother must be brought to judgment. If he abuses his brother he must answer for it to the court; if he sneers at him he will have to answer for it in the fires of hell" (Matthew 5:22, NEB)? How can we increase our appreciation of people of other nationalities?

DISCIPLINES THAT CHANGE THINGS

Mrs. Thad Gibson knows how severe the grip of depression can be. For weeks she wept and felt helpless; barely able to get through each day, she was afraid to be left alone for fear that she would kill herself, and when she went to bed she often hoped that she would never wake up.

Then she heard about an unusual experiment. Some of the members of the Sunday-school class she attended became interested in a "Brave Christians Experiment," which offered the hope of changing one's life. Mrs. Gibson took a copy of the plan home and began following the suggestions. Today, she says, "I am a changed person. Now I can cope with whatever must be coped with. Letting God be the center of your life puts things in the proper perspective, and nothing is unbearable."

Complete information about the plan that changed Mrs. Gibson's life is available from Brave Christian Associates, Box 987, Tallahassee, Florida 32301. In brief, she agreed to follow these five disciplines:

1. Spend one half hour each morning in prayer and meditation.

2. Give God one tenth of your earnings.

3. Give God two hours of your time each week.

4. Meet once a week to pray with others in the plan.

5. Witness to others about your experiences.

The daily half hour of devotions required by the Brave Christians Experiment is carefully programed. The first ten minutes are spent reading and meditating on one of the Scriptural passages the Experiment provides for each day in the month. These consist of II Chronicles 7:14, Mark 11:24, Psalm 66:18, John 14:27, and other specially chosen verses. The worshiper writes in his own words how the passage applies to his life.

The second ten minutes are spent planning a completely unselfish act of kindness toward someone, and writing down in detail what is to be done. The plan must be carried out that day.

The final ten minutes are spent writing out how the worshiper wishes to build up his life, thoughtfully and prayerfully.

When the plan is carried out as specified, amazing results have followed. After a month of the Experiment, one man testified that he was no longer an alcoholic.

Religion is often so vague and formless that it makes only the most superficial impression on an individual's life. When it is presented in specific, clear-cut steps like those in the Brave Christians Experiment, it often gets specific, clear-cut results.

Are specific disciplines or rules necessary in Christianity? Does religion have value if it never seems to accomplish anything specific? Could the Brave Christians Experiment help you, or someone you know?

DRINKING AND DRIVING

There is no question but that a high proportion of traffic accidents are caused by drivers who have had one or several too many drinks. Some states are doing something to decrease the mayhem. New Jersey, for example, has a sobriety test: If you are involved in an accident, your breath is tested for alcoholic content; if you refuse the test, you lose your license for six months; if you have not been overdrinking, the test shows it; if you have been overdrinking, you may lose your license for as long as two years. Before the law was passed, less than three thousand drivers in New Jersey had been convicted of drunken driving. Four years later, more than nine thousand drinkers had been removed from the state's roads.

We think New Jersey's example should be followed nationally. It is shocking to know that a thousand people are killed on our highways *every week* while we do nothing to stop the slaughter. Reducing the number of drunks behind wheels would be one of the most effective ways to keep the Commandment, "You shall not kill."

Where does personal liberty end and public responsibility begin? Would you fly on an airline that permitted pilots to drink on duty? Or one that killed a thousand passengers a week? Is our age too mechanized to allow drinking?

See also ALCOHOL AND COMMON SENSE, ALCOHOLISM.

DRUGS: LSD and Art Linkletter's Daughter

One of the tragic events of 1969 was what happened to Art Linkletter's daughter Diane. She had experimented with taking LSD, her father said, and had confided to him that the whole thing was ridiculous. Frightened by the experience and by the "bum trips" of friends, she vowed never to try LSD again. But hallucinations kept recurring until, depressed and afraid she was losing her mind, she leaped from her apartment to her death.

Shaken by the horrible happening, Linkletter told of his daughter's experience to a bipartisan drug-discussion group at the White House. "Diane was not a hippie," he said. "She was not a drug addict. She was not a nutty girl. She had everything to live for. . . . The point is that the kids of America today are reacting to the drug society in which they have grown up. From the time they are born they see on the television tube everybody popping things into their mouths, whether they want to get thin, fat, or happy, or go to sleep or wake up or erase tension or take away headaches or whatever. So they are used to putting chemicals, and seeing everybody putting chemicals, into their body.

"Then when you add to that the normal teen-age and the upper teen-age desire to do something daring . . . something a little bit against the law or against rules . . . they want the kicks that come from chemicals."

What can be done? Linkletter said that just as we teach children not to walk in front of cars, we should teach them at a very early age never to put anything but food or prescribed medicine into their mouths, and never under any condition to inject anything into their blood streams. "It is just a plain, simple statement of fact, rather than a 'no-no' or a moralism. I think we should make the next generation understand what they are putting into their blood is not an answer to life's problems. It only exaggerates and accentuates them."

How heavily do we rely on drugs and pills? If every headache, problem, or bit of tension drives us to one bottle or another, what does this teach our children? Are all these chemicals necessary for us? Certain religious groups insist on as simple a life as possible, from clothing to eating habits. Would it be good if more of us followed such a rule, and applied it to drugs?

What is the best way to train young people toward mature, responsible, Christian living? Can formal religious education do the job? Are drugs a problem in themselves or the symptom of a deeper problem? If so, what? How does our faith point to an answer?

DRUGS AND TELEVISION

"How can any institution [like school] . . . compare with the force of television on the mind of a child? We are told that the average family watches television five and a half hours a day. Thus, if a city child begins serious watching when he is two, then by the time he comes into our schools he has seen 8000 hours of television.

"And what has he been taught? He has been taught to relax minor tensions with a pill; to take off weight with a pill; to win status and sophistication with a cigarette; to wake up, slow down, be happy, relieve tension with pills—that is, with drugs."

So said New York's Mayor John V. Lindsay in a speech, on February 7, 1970, concerning the city's program of education against drug addiction in the schools.[1]

If we have brought up a drug-prone generation, what can we do to reverse the situation? One researcher says he does not permit his children to watch more than one hour of television a day. Are we helping our children when we turn our television sets into baby sitters? What kind of example do we give our children by the things we pop into our mouths for all sorts of purposes? Should television be used to fight drug addiction? Should some commercials be restricted or prohibited?

EDUCATION: Instant Answers?

Twentieth-century Americans are accustomed to instant answers to questions. Somewhere, we feel, there must be a computer big enough to tell us what we want to know, this moment.

Some things, however, don't work like that. When a marriage has been deteriorating for years, it may take years to restore it to health. A good teacher needs more than a five-minute survey of the lesson. When plans were announced for the United Methodist Christian Educators Fellowship for 1970, it was specified that this would not be the kind of meeting at which you sit, listen to lectures, and go home with a bag full of printed leaflets and a few notes. No: "The city of San Francisco itself (site of the conference) will be the learning center," it was announced. Participants in the conference were to be given tape recorders and sent out into the city. A resource

[1] Quoted in the New York *Times,* February 8, 1970.

center was planned "complete with collections of films, tapes, videotapes, television, pictures, printed papers, exhibits of art, music, and personal-experience reports."

Rev. Richard L. Cookson, chairman of the design team for the conference, said: "We are trying to free people from the image that all they need for a conference is to bring together a group of experts to 'turn them on' and they will have instant answers to the questions and needs of people."

Certainly there is a place for the report of the expert who has spent years struggling with a problem. But unless we too have done some wrestling with the same kind of problem, how can we either appreciate his findings, know whether to accept them, or profit from them? Sometimes one is forced to the conclusion that the only real teacher is experience. When I have learned something from my own trials and errors, I do not forget it. Perhaps this age of the television camera and the tape recorder will help free us from an unhealthy dependence on books alone, bring us back into closer contact with the real world, and help educators learn how the mystery of education takes place.

Are there instant answers to any really important problems? Which makes the better teacher: the person who knows all the latest educational techniques, or the person who loves his subject and his pupils? How much time should a Sunday-school teacher give, on an average, to a lesson? Can a teacher teach anything effectively if the learner is not voluntarily putting forth all his effort to learn? Does the learning process need teachers? What is their role?

ESSENTIALS: What Are They?

Jerzy Grotowski is a Polish experimentalist in the theater. As a young man he asked himself what the theater really is: What makes it different from motion pictures or television? Then he began to strip away everything that could be removed from drama, experimenting without stage scenery, without costuming, without elaborate lighting. He concentrated on what seemed to be the irreducible essentials: speaking, breathing, gesture. And spectators at Grotowski's productions are often overwhelmed by the power of these simplicities.

In education we used to assume that the proper buildings, the correct administrative procedures, the latest in equipment were essential. Today there are schools without walls, classes without paid instructors or roll call, curricula without any of the traditional structure or requirements. In such settings, students are often surprised to learn that learning is exciting and fun, and educators learn that the students often learn faster and more efficiently without the usual trappings. The Parkway Program of Philadelphia is one such experiment. More than 10,000 students tried to get into it in the 1969–70 season (there was room for only 500). One girl said about the program, "There's no attitude like, 'It's just another stupid fifteen-year-old, so what's the difference!' "

No good teacher, of course, treats his students as stupid. But some young people believe their teachers have such an attitude, and it is a victory for education when the pupils do not so believe.

The churches, too, are experimenting with all kinds of new forms. New Catholic churches are doing away with statuary and crucifixes, moving the altar into the center of the building, modernizing their liturgy, and bringing laymen into the decision-making processes of the church. There are Protestant congregations without buildings or paid ministers, worship services without any of the traditional structures, religious bodies rethinking their purposes and strategies.

What is really essential for a church? What would happen to your church if it functioned for a month without flowers or a choir or the use of its building? Would it survive? Would it grow stronger or weaker as a result?

What is Christian education all about? Are lesson books and quarterlies, filmstrips and attendance records necessary? Would religious training be possible without such things?

What are the essentials of life? What are the things you

could not live without? How many of these does the Bible emphasize, and how many does it warn us not to get too firmly attached to?

What would you give your life for?

ETERNITY

An unknown versifier wrote:

> The stars shall live for a million years,
>   A million years and a day,
> But God and I will live and love
>   When the stars have passed away.

A thought something like that is found in an ancient document from another unknown author:

> Thou, Lord, in the beginning
> hast laid the foundation of the earth;
> and the heavens are the works of thy hands.
> They shall perish, but thou remainest:
> and they all shall wax old as doth a garment;
> and as a vesture shalt thou fold them up,
> and they shall be changed:
> but thou art the same,
> and thy years shall not fail.

> *(Hebrews 1:10–12)*

Picture God folding up the universe, taking down the stars like someone discarding used clothing! The universe will grow old and run down, but God cannot change. We speak of someone's "passing away," but the New Testament says that "the world passeth away" while "he that doeth the will of God abideth forever" (I John 2:17).

What is eternal life? Is it a matter of time, or of something beyond time and space? Does John 17:3 throw light on this? What should Christians fear? Anything?

See also DEATH AND RESURRECTION, IMMORTALITY.

The following advertisement was clipped from a college newspaper.

WOULD YOU LIKE TO BECOME A MINISTER?

ORDINATION is without question and for life. LEGAL in all 50 states and most foreign countries. Perform legal marriages, ordinations and funerals. Receive discounts on some fares. Over 265,000 ministers have already been ordained. Minister's credentials and license sent; an ordainment certificate for framing and an ID card for your billfold. We need your help to cover mailing, handling, and administration costs. Your generous contribution is appreciated. ENCLOSE A FREE WILL OFFERING.

Write to: ——————

Most churches, of course, require an intensive course of study in addition to college before ordination is granted.

Why are college students singled out for this ad? Is ordination being offered as an easy way to avoid the draft? Should periodicals accept advertising of this kind? Should the government prohibit it? Does the government have a right to pass on the requirements for ordination? If not, does anyone?

Some clergymen have a poor reputation for paying bills. What kind of witness is this? Does it have any relation to the fact that many ministers are going into debt, and are paid less than any other group with similar educational background? Should clergymen be expected to be more honest or more ethical than ordinary Christians? Why or why not? How do the ethics of Christians compare with those of other people? How should they compare?

EVERYDAY CHRISTIANITY: "Blessings from Below"

A list of diabolical beatitudes was printed in a rally program of North Association Women of the American Baptist churches of New Jersey. Although they are attributed to Satan, no permission has been secured from that personage for publication here.

BLESSINGS FROM BELOW

"Blessed are they who are bored with the minister's mannerisms and mistakes; for they get nothing out of the sermon. Blessed are they who are not interested in the affairs of the church; for they cause the world to say, 'The church is failing.'

Blessed are they who gossip; for they cause strife and division which pleases me very much.

Blessed are they who are easily offended; for they soon get angry and quit.

Blessed is he who professes to love God but hates his brother; for he shall be with me forever.

Blessed are the troublemakers; for they shall be called the children of the devil.

Blessed is he who has no time to pray; for he shall be easy prey."

—Satan"

What is your reaction? How does church attendance relate to everyday Christianity? Which is better: not to attend church, or to come and criticize? How does the church help us live? What do our actions do to, or for, the church? What is Christianity?

See also DAILY LIFE AND OUR FAITH, FAITH AND EVERYDAY WORK, CHRISTIANITY.

FAITH AND EVERYDAY WORK: Could a Convinced Buddhist Work Here?

The Dakota Project is a frightening novel about a super-secret government project. Signing up as a technical writer for the Project, Dick Conroy finds himself behind barbed wire, under constant surveillance, and involved in work the purpose of which he can only guess—until he stumbles on the horrifying truth. Part of his job on the Project is to plan an advertising campaign for a new food product in Oriental countries which have food taboos. "The campaign should imply . . . that Product X is (a) not prohibited to Moslems, since it contains no pork; (b) not offensive to Hindus, since it contains no beef."

What *does* the new food, Product X, contain? Dick begins to suspect it is human flesh. "Could a convinced Buddhist go on working here, in the Project?" he muses. "Hard to believe. A devout Christian?"[1]

The present Secretary General of the United Nations is a devout Buddhist who begins every day with meditation. His dedicated work for world peace has earned him the admiration and respect of millions of people. Could a dedicated Buddhist do everything some Christians do? Does it matter where a person works, in relation to his faith? How much of our everyday life does our faith have a right to influence—or "interfere with"? Could a convinced Buddhist do your job?

See also DAILY LIFE AND OUR FAITH.

FINANCING THE CHURCH: Chile's Way

If your church received a large amount of its support from valuable real estate, substantial endowments, shrewd financial manipulations, and gifts from wealthy families, wouldn't you be happy?

Romans Catholics in Chile aren't. Although much of their church income came from such sources, including land grants going back to colonial times and endowments whose value has multiplied over many years, church leaders are renouncing it all as they plan to rely instead on regular contributions from the members. Most of the members, reports the *National Register* for January 18, 1970, are poor; the average Chilean earns

[1] Jack Beeching, *The Dakota Project* (Delacorte Press, 1969).

94

just $385 a year. But even though the members can only supply 10 percent of its needs, the Chilean church plans to take this daring step and to turn over all its financial affairs to lay groups.

What the church in Chile has in mind is discouraging expensive weddings and funerals, making these and other services available at low cost or without fee, aiding local community needs, and making all the members aware of their obligations to help. Some of the clergy, realizing that the new plan may be difficult to launch, are willing to take secular jobs if necessary to make ends meet.

The Spirit of God appears to be working in marvelous ways today in all kinds of churches throughout the world. What is he saying to your church? To you? What is the real purpose of the church? What part should money play in achieving this? Is it healthy for any church to rely on a few individuals or sources for most of its income? Is this good for the other members?

Can Protestants learn anything from present-day Catholics?

FOREIGN AID: For What?

One of the things to which American politicians often point with pride is the amount of money we officially give other countries. In its issues of May 27 and October 7, 1969, *Look* magazine published Christopher S. Wren's reports on the incredible tortures by which the government of Greece tries to frighten its citizens into submission. People suspected of opposing this brutal dictatorship are hung by their feet, deprived of food and water, beaten until their feet swell up and are broken. They are tortured with electrical charges and sexually molested. And the torture is identified with the United States, which gives the Greek Government forty million dollars a year in foreign aid. *Look* asks, "Why should we hand over American taxpayers' money to a government that rules by torture?"

Why, indeed? It is good to help nations in need, but why

is it that so often the governments we support happen to be *bloody dictatorships? Why should our money be used to crush the revolts of those who are trying to overthrow their evil rulers? And why should it be used to perpetuate monstrous tyranny?*

Some people care what happens to their tax money. Do we? Do we do anything about it? What should we do?

See also AMERICAN FOREIGN AID, INTERNATIONAL RELATIONSHIPS.

FREE ENTERPRISE AND GOVERNMENT CONTROLS

One of the finer, but also one of the more conservative, newspapers in the United States is the *Christian Science Monitor*. Both its news columns and its editorial opinions are usually balanced, restrained, weighted more on the side of the status quo than radical reform. In his column in the *Monitor* on February 3, 1970, Joseph C. Harsch told of a businessman who sat through a discussion of pollution and other dangers to our environment and finally asked, "Does all this mean more government interference in business, and higher taxes?"

It does. Under a Republican President, the United States is beginning to take actions that may more deeply affect "free enterprise" than did those actions of a Republican President named Theodore Roosevelt. It will have to take such actions, if there is to be a future for human life.

Harsch reminds us that "totally 'free private enterprise,' as this highly unscientific term is understood in the United States, is not a system or condition ordained by the Creator.

"It is, in fact," he says, "a residual survival from an unusual and unrepeatable phase in the conquest of this planet by men. . . .

"The men who thrust forth from Europe and swarmed over the new continents broke away from a highly controlled economic system. . . . 'Free enterprise' as known in the United States of Warren Harding was a leftover from the time when men escaped from the organized society of the seventeenth and eighteenth centuries, and did as they pleased.

"The result has been a period of history in which the interests of the manufacturer and merchandiser took precedence over the interests of just plain people."

Those interests took precedence too long, says Mr. Harsch. They have so damaged our environment that they threaten human survival, and they must be stopped. We have to agree.

How free is "free enterprise"? Why has American business so consistently refused to enter a free world market, but instead has kept "foreign" goods from competing, through high tariffs? If the people cannot protect themselves from the ruination of their beaches, their streams, their forests, their national resources, and the very air they breathe through collective government action, how can they survive? How are we to strike the right balance between business interests, labor interests, government interests, and the interests of the people at large? Is there any one easy answer?

FREEDOM: For Whom?

The organization Freedoms Foundation lists among others these rights of "the American way of life":

Right to worship God in one's own way.

Right to free speech and press.

Right to peaceable assembly.

Right to privacy in our homes.

Right of habeas corpus—no excessive bail.

Right to trial by jury—innocent until proved guilty.

Right to move about freely at home and abroad.

Right to bargain with our employers and employees.

Right to bargain for goods and services in a free market.

Right to the service of government as a protector and referee.

Right to freedom from arbitary government regulation and control

Do these rights apply to Black Muslims as well as white Baptists and Methodists? To Black Panthers as well as Masons, Republicans, and Democrats? To workingmen as well as businessmen? To young people as well as old? To the poor as well as the well-to-do? The Supreme Court has sought to maintain many of these rights in our nation. Are we, too, concerned about guarding these basic freedoms for everyone?

FREEDOM: Of Opinion

"Everyone has the right to freedom of opinion and expression; this right includes freedom to hold opinions without interference and to seek, receive and impart information and ideas through any media regardless of frontiers."—United Nations Universal Declaration of Human Rights, Article 19.

Do we believe that? With what restrictions? In recent years various countries have forbidden travel into certain other countries, and have even prohibited literature from "taboo" areas. Such restrictions seem to be easing. Is this good or bad? When Premier Khrushchev was interviewed on American television, there was considerable protest that he was permitted to be heard. Thereupon the television networks began a policy of following political speeches with commentary, to give a "balanced" view. This practice was denounced in 1969 by Vice-President Agnew on the grounds that a speech by President Nixon was distorted before people had a chance to understand it.

Would it be better if we heard only one side of a question? Should criticism of American officials be forbidden, as is the case in some countries? What is the value of freedom of speech and of the media of communication?

FREEDOM, TRUE

In a radio message, Dr. David Allan Hubbard, president of Fuller Theological Seminary, told of the times he used to travel with his father through fog so thick the driver could scarcely see two feet ahead. His older brother Paul often had to get out of the car and hold a flashlight on the edge of the road so that they could move ahead.

Dr. Hubbard likened the fog to the confusion in today's values, morality, choices. He said the word of God comes like that light to give direction and true freedom:

"Christian freedom is not freedom to ad lib or to free-lance. . . . We are not free to fumble and grope our way through life. Freedom is not the liberty to move through a cafeteria line of worldly values and to eat whatever we want. True freedom is relief from entangling reliances on selfishness and apathy so that we can begin to obey God. The social nature of life tells us that we must have standards to avoid confusion. Why not take these standards from the one that knows us best, the one who has the most at stake in our lives, who gave himself for us in Jesus Christ that we might know the true meaning of life?"

How free is freedom? What freedom is there for anyone when a driver breaks all the rules of the road? How does freedom fit in with Christian responsibility? Which is more truly free: a weathervane or a rocket?

For reference: John 8:36; James 1:25; Galatians 5:1; Ephesians 6:6.

FREEDOM AND FAITH

Early in 1970 the government of South Africa dropped its charges against twenty-two black youths, in a trial which followed several months of detention and investigation with two months of court action. As soon as the charges were dropped, however, the young Africans were rearrested under the terms of a law—the Terrorism Act—which allows those accused to remain without trial in indefinite detention.

A white Protestant minority rules South Africa.

Does it grace the Christian faith for a group of white Chris-

*tians to suppress the natives of the land they took from them?
Is it a testimony to the love of Christ for these professing
Christians to move the natives onto "farms" so dry and rocky
they look like the desert by the Dead Sea? Is it even human or
decent in any sense for this white minority to practice cruel
and unusual acts of terror and intimidation against the black
majority who rightfully owned the land of South Africa in the
first place?*

*A dedicated group of Christians, including such renowned
world leaders as Alan Paton, do not think so. They have
faced trial, imprisonment, and the possibility of torture and
death in their stand for Christ against a powerful branch of
the church. How should Christians behave when they control
a society?*

FREEDOM AND SILENCE

One of the great differences usually pointed out between
communism and democracy is freedom. But what is freedom?

It is defined and guaranteed by our Constitution—specifically, by the Bill of Rights, which specifies that every citizen
has these rights: freedom of religion, freedom of speech,
freedom of the press, and the right "peaceably to assemble
and to petition the government for a redress of grievances."

Several times, however, in the late 1960s, when American
citizens exercised their constitutional freedoms to say what
they thought about the country's military policies, they were
ridiculed and intimidated by certain government officials. When
the largest political gathering in American history peaceably
assembled in Washington, D.C., in mid-November, 1969, to
demonstrate the concern of millions of Americans for peace
and justice, some officials belittled the gathering, and uttered
veiled threats against the American press and news media.

At the Washington Moratorium Senator George McGovern
spoke:

". . . Let no American be frightened out of his constitutional rights. Let no teacher or student, no preacher or politician, no journalist or television commentator, be silenced by fear.

"Let me put it to you plainly. A dangerous effort is underway to confuse, divide, and intimidate the American people, and especially our news commentators. When the great television networks and a distinguished elder statesman are assaulted by the chief executives of the land, no citizen is safe. Liberty itself is endangered. That is not the method of this peaceful assembly and that is not the method that made America. So I plead again with every citizen of this great land—and especially with those in television and in the press on whom we depend for information—do not let them scare you into silence."

Can we retain our rights if we are afraid to exercise them? How does freedom of speech and the press help guarantee the freedom of democracy? Is freedom good or bad? If good, should we be frightened into silence? How does freedom relate to our faith? What does Galatians 5:1 mean to you?

THE FUTURE: The End or the Beginning?

The mushrooming dangers of harmful additives in our food, pesticides in our water, pollution in our air, overpopulation on our planet, have produced studies and conferences in all parts of the earth. Late in 1969 Daniel Moynihan, President Richard Nixon's urban-affairs adviser, said that in view of all this, "we may have even less than a fifty-fifty chance of living until 1980." Early in 1970 the Church of England debated several of these problems. Canon Hugh Montefiore, a distinguished Anglican clergyman who was born in the Jewish faith, commented:

"I do not wish to be so alarmist, but it must be said that Christians who live in a New Testament perspective can hardly be surprised if civilized life is drawing to its close."

At almost the same time, an American biologist, Dr. Albert Szent-Gyorgi, said, "At present we are on the road to extermination."

What is the solution?

"There is no solution to my mind," said Dr. Szent-Gyorgi. ". . . The only way we can survive is to make a new beginning." The biologist expressed the hope that young people might be flexible enough to discover some new ideas that will enable life on earth to survive.

Canon Montefiore called for worldwide cooperation to cope with the worldwide problems threatening men and animals.

Is the end of mankind near? Certainly we cannot continue ignoring the laws of the universe except at the gravest peril. Says Christian leader Bruce Larson, however: "It may be that our whole field of eschatology is wrong. Rather than living in 'the last days,' we may be living in the initial stages of the Christian Era. It is quite possible that God in his infinite love and patience has allowed mankind two thousand years in the laboratory of life to come up with a working blueprint or a few working models of 'the new being' and 'the new Jerusalem' that Christ made possible by his invasion of the world. Perhaps we are not merely witnessing a great new reformation of the church in our time, but the beginning of what God had in mind for man when he allowed the cosmic Christ to become the man Jesus just twenty centuries ago."[1]

Is the choice up to us? If we look at our problems with common sense and faith, is it possible God will open new vistas of hope and discovery before us? Could it be that he is now preparing both the church and the world to face their failures and to find the way through love, trust, respect, and cooperation? Are we willing to face up to our dangers so that we can embark upon a new beginning?

GAMBLING ADDICTS: Gamblers Anonymous

People who gamble, like people who drink, can become addicts. Victims of the gambling habit, like alcoholics, often use the habit to escape from severe emotional problems that usually

[1] *Faith At Work,* January 1970.

began in their childhood and resulted in lives acutely disordered. Except that in neither case does the escape work; it compounds the problems.

Gamblers Anonymous is an organization made up of those who have kicked the gambling compulsion and are helping others to do the same. Nationally headquartered at Box 17173, Los Angeles, California 90017, it has chapters in most large cities.

"Most GA members," wrote David Holmstrom in the *Christian Science Monitor* (January 13, 1970), ". . . say that a knowledge of why they gambled is not helpful in their efforts to end their gambling." In his article on the group he quoted two principles from the organization's handbook. One is that "people with like problems can be helpful to each other." Another is that help "can be effective only when it is asked for and open-mindedly accepted." Members have found it is a waste of time to try to force the program on anyone who is not ready to seek and accept help.

Holmstrom said that "the crucial element on the road back to normalcy is the personal contact with compulsive gamblers who are 'clean,' or struggling to be clean."

Does all that say anything to the church?

Christians sometimes look askance at organizations such as Alcoholics Anonymous or Gamblers Anonymous. Why? Shouldn't we thank God when any group can help someone in need? On one occasion the disciples said to Jesus, "Teacher, we saw a man casting out demons in your name, and we forbade him, because he was not following us." He answered, "Do not forbid him . . . he that is not against us is for us" (Mark 9:38-40). Some churches provide a place for AAs to meet; why shouldn't all churches welcome such groups?

Religious education is important, but shouldn't the experience of Gamblers Anonymous make it clear that knowledge alone doesn't turn a person around, or help much when he is gripped by a desperate problem? *Personal contact,* however, does.

If it takes people with similar problems to help each other, should we expect to be much help to someone whose back-

*ground is completely different from ours? In such a case, why
not try to put him in contact with someone who has traveled
on a similar road?*

*Finally, is it possible that Gamblers Anonymous can teach
us that there is a time and a place for everything? How
many good intentions are wasted on those who have no interest
in what is being offered, or are not ready to ask for help
and receive it?*

For reference: Luke 8:4-15.

GOALS: Do We Have Them?

During the 1950s the United States gave considerable attention to its goals. Conferences were held, papers were read,
and when it was all over, some people wondered if this great
nation had somehow lost its way. For there was almost complete
disagreement over what our national goals should be, whether
our goals were stated in the Constitution, whether we needed
completely new ones, or whether it was possible for a nation
to have any.

In the January 19, 1970, *Newsweek,* Stewart Alsop wrote
of the unrest among Japanese university students: "In Japan—
as increasingly in the United States—two separate and hostile
cultures have grown up. . . . 'In postwar Japan,' said a professor, 'Marxist dogma has been absolutely dominant in education circles.'

"The beautiful simplicities of Marxist dogma have exerted
their familiar appeal to young minds. 'The Marxists have a
strict goal,' said an earnest girl student. 'So it is easy to be
a Marxist. We who are not Marxists need a strict goal, but
we cannot find it.' "

It's easy to accept a simplistic goal like the Marxists': Get
rid of capitalism so the millennium of socialism will solve all
the problems. Sensible people know that even if Marxism
worked, life isn't that simple. But is there any goal at all?

How would you as a Christian define a realistic goal for your country? Or for yourself?

In his great poem "Locksley Hall," Alfred Tennyson wrote:

Yet I doubt not through the ages one increasing purpose runs,
And the thoughts of men are widened with the process of
the suns.

Is there a purpose running through the ages? What did some of the great prophets see as a world goal?

For reference: Isaiah 2:1–4; 11:1–9; Zechariah 8:1–8; 9:10; Revelation 22:1–5.

GOD: Alive and Active

"Either there is no God at all—or he walks beside us as we travel through this wonderful, beautiful, confusing journey we call life. I am sure I have felt his presence at the conference table in Rome when as Hindu, Moslem, Buddhist, Jew, Christian and atheist we laid aside our beliefs or nonbelief, and the starving children of the world became not little wards of any one country or any one religion but simply God's children looking at us with pleading eyes for food. I have glimpsed his joy in creation through the eyes of a peasant farmer harvesting a bountiful crop from soil that at one time yielded only a pittance. I have seen his righteous anger in the wrath of a little Indian woman standing up in a world conference at Washington and defying weak-kneed men who were trying to equivocate on her resolution for the need of birth control in a world with more people than it can feed. His mercy is seen in the healing of the leper, in the cooling of the brow of the fever-stricken. You can see his dignity in the upright bearing of a man who has at last learned to read and to sign his own name. . . .

"Strange, isn't it, that in a day when we hear rumors of the death of God, the Judeo-Christian principles of social action, set out in their noblest form by his Son, have received a worldwide acceptance on a scale and at a rate no one ever dreamed would be possible."[1]

Is God dead? How could you convince someone else of his reality? What is more convincing than his works of love and mercy, his cause of truth and justice, his concern for peace and brotherhood, through people?

GOD: The One Who Died

"If God is dead as some have contended, then it's probably just as well to let him lie there. I fancy he wasn't big enough for the job anyway. Especially if it's that tiresome old God of middle-class morality. He was nearly as dull as the Victorian God before him who banned sex. Certainly if he isn't big enough to incorporate the advances of science, then it's best to let him pass on, poor thing.

"However, the God who is *God* is not apart from life drawing us to him, but is in all of life, at work in it, at work with us, alive. He constantly confronts us with truth, and if it happens to be a truth that is against our religion, then we will have to bring the religion into line. For God compels us to honesty—to the kind of ruthless telling-of-the-truth which alone can bridge the awful gap between polite religiosity and the Real.

"So if you've just laid to rest some cumbersome God who's been in your hair, who's been directing you against your common sense and better judgment and deepest constructive instincts, who's urged you to be more religious rather than seeing to it that you become more human, more authentic, and more real, well, then, give him a nice little burial and then let's get on with it. Get hooked into the life before you, walk the path under your feet, for that's where God is, 'closer to you than breathing, nearer than hands and feet.' "[2]

[1] Dr. Howard L. Trueman, "Don't Tell *Me* That God Is Dead," *United Church Observer*, October 15, 1969. Used by permission.
[2] Emily A. Swinnerton. Used by permission of the author.

What God could die except some false god who never existed anyway except in someone's imagination? Do you agree that the true God puts truth and honesty even ahead of "religious" ceremonies? Is there a gap between "polite religiosity and the Real"? Does God want us to be more religious? or more real and human and authentic persons?

GOD: WHO OR WHAT? The Meaning of "Yahweh"

In her fine little book entitled *Psalms '70*, Mary Perkins Ryan mentions the new awareness of God she received as she moved out from the cloistered protection of her church's ancient practices, into the streets and the battles of the age. "Even though in praying I still say, 'Lord,' from long habit, it does not seem to express my new awareness of the 'Wholly Otherness' of God and of the wonder of his concern for human persons and human history."

Then she refers to Moses' vision of the burning bush, through which God revealed himself by a new name: "Yahweh," or "I am who I am." "In other words, Yahweh is the God who is beyond all our formulations, who nonetheless reveals himself in human history, sending men on missions of deliverance to their fellows, missions in which he will be with them. Addressing God by this strange 'personal name,' at least now and then, seems to help eat through layers of both too philosophical and too domesticated ways of approaching God, and to be a reminder of whom we are daring to speak to, because he has first spoken to us and given us work to do."[1]

What have you found helpful in approaching God in prayer? Do you agree that our concept of "God" may be too philosophical to represent him truly? And that the word "Lord" may be too domesticated, palsy, familiar, for the God of Scripture and of life? To some of us, "Yahweh" sounds strange, too. Does Mrs. Ryan's explanation help you?

[1] *Psalms '70* (Pflaum Press), pp. 19–20.

GOD AND MAN TODAY: Is There a Message From Beyond?

In his poetically haunting book *The Unexpected Universe,* scientist Loren Eiseley warns us that science does not have all the answers: "The wild reality always eludes our grasp." Further, he says that human beings are "message carriers" who have spent all history trying to remember some "further instruction" which remains just beyond the level of their consciousness.

Is that message, that further instruction, a word from the God who made us for himself and will never be content (as we can never be) until we find our contentment in him? Is it possible that somewhere back in history, man fell from a higher state of wisdom and that part of the reason for the chaos and lostness he finds everywhere today is that he is struggling vainly to remember what it was like in a long-lost garden of blessedness and fulfillment?

In the *Phaedo,* Plato remarks how difficult it is to attain certainty about anything. Still, he says, a man should either discover the truth, or take the best and most indisputable theory he can find and use it like a raft on which to sail through life—"if he cannot find some word of God which will more surely and safely carry him."

Is there a sure word from God? Where and what is it? What certainties does it offer? What use should we make of God's word?

GOOD AND EVIL: Don't Forget the Small Good Things

"Sometimes one is led to believe that the world continues to exist by virtue of the small good things that go on despite the pain and the ugliness that surround us, and that violence itself is possible only against a background of tiny, anchored normalcies. If all was violence, the world would disintegrate."[1]

[1] Chaim Potok in *The Ladies' Home Journal,* December 1969, p. 134.

We forget all the small good things in life because we take them for granted, and the bad things make such an impression. Several times I have lost things—a briefcase, a ring of keys, a bankbook—which later were found and returned by a complete stranger. The robberies and kidnappings make news because they are so rare; when good things make headlines, it will be time to leave for some other part of the universe.

We need to be aware of reality, but we also need to remember that life is fundamentally good, and to concentrate on the right things. "Finally, brethren," wrote St. Paul from his damp prison cell, "whatsoever things are true, whatsoever things are just, whatsoever things are pure, whatsoever things are lovely, whatsoever things are of good report; if there be any virtue, and if there be any praise, think on these things" (Philippians 4:8).

GROWTH: Earth the Center of the Universe?

Our most unusual Christmas card was a reprint of an astronomical chart from the fifteenth century. Around the earth revolved the moon, the sun, the planets, and the constellations of the Zodiac, all in gorgeous colors.

Today that diagram looks ridiculous, but for the fifteenth century it was a genuine scientific achievement. It explained the heavens within the framework of everything known at the time. Today it is outdated, but how many of today's unquestioned scientific facts will stand up in 2001? The rocks our spacemen have brought from the moon have already exploded a number of cherished theories about the earth and the moon and their history.

Growth is important, whether in science or in faith. Jesus as a child "grew, and waxed strong in spirit, filled with wisdom" (Luke 2:40). Everything living has to grow. Is your faith greater today than ten years ago? Is your conception of God grander and more glorious? Have you outgrown some childish thing in your life, as St. Paul did (I Corinthians 13:11)?

Is your social conscience abreast of present-day events? Can it be said of you, as it was of Jesus (Luke 2:52), that there is measurable growth "in wisdom and stature, and in favor with God and man"?

HANDICAPS: Dominate Them

To many of us, becoming blind or deaf would be an unthinkable disaster. Yet David Wright in his book *Deafness* says that the deaf person can be in a strong psychological position. "Though this is only true of those who have dominated, not merely accepted, the disability. Every disability offers the same alternative: Either it dominates you or you dominate it."

The natural first reaction to a crushing problem is shock, hopelessness, bitterness, rebellion. So Job felt when multiple disasters entered his life. But Job wrestled through his doubts and depression, and finally came to the point where he could say of God, "Though he slay me, yet will I trust him."

How do you come out on top of disasters or disabilities? What place does faith have in overcoming problems? What Bible characters, or other persons, have refused to be dominated by their circumstances but instead dominated them?

How can I help the nearest handicapped person I know? What does and should the government do for the handicapped? What should industry do? The church?

HANDS: What Do They Communicate?

Our hands speak—especially to a blind person. Helen Keller, America's tremendously gifted conqueror of handicaps, writes:

"The hands of those I meet are dumbly eloquent to me. I have met people so empty of joy that when I clasped their frosty fingertips it seemed as if I were shaking hands with a northeast storm. Others there are whose hands have sunbeams in them, so that their grasp warms my heart. It may be only the clinging touch of a child's hand, but there is as much potential sunshine in it for me as there is in a loving glance for others."

What do our hands say by what they do? What kind of spirit is being communicated through our bodies? What can others know of us but what we say through our eyes, our faces, our hands, our posture, our deeds?

HATE: Is It Masculine?

In his recent biography, *Huey Long,* T. Harry Williams says of the Louisiana politician, ". . . a normal masculine emotion never appeared in him—that occasional red rage which makes a man want to fling himself at the throat of another man." And he quotes Long's statement that he did not fight in World War I "because I was not mad at anybody over there."

Is it "normal" or "masculine" to want to fling yourself at someone's throat, or to desire to stick a bayonet through someone's liver? Does a soldier prove he is "a man" when he dares not refuse to go with his buddies to the nearest whorehouse? Do we need new ideas of what is "masculine," what is "feminine," and what is "normal" and "abnormal"? Animals kill one another only for food, and never their own kind (except rats). When a man enjoys torturing or lynching or shooting his fellow men, is he normal, or subanimal?

HEROISM

Harrison Kohler was with the American forces in Vietnam when his unit came across a wounded enemy soldier. The company radioed a Green Beret officer, "Captain W.," whose troops Kohler's men had to work with. Captain W. was supposed to interrogate the prisoner.

"I sat down for a few minutes," reported Kohler in the January 28, 1970, *Christian Century,* "and then I heard several shots. Word was quickly passed down that Captain W., unable to get any information from the prisoner, had shot him." That night Kohler talked with two men who had seen the murder. Captain W., they said, had filled the legs and abdomen of the wounded prisoner with bullets and then left him lying there bleeding. On being asked about this, Captain W. said, "He'll die."

Later, Captain W. was awarded one of the highest awards of the United States Government, the Distinguished Service Cross, for his "heroic actions" during the time of the shooting of the Vietnamese prisoner. Kohler kept the newspaper clipping about Captain W.'s award for one reason: "If I ever had to listen to pious rhetoric about war, I could always take out the clipping and refresh my memory."

What is heroism? Which takes more real bravery: to kill an unarmed military prisoner, or to obey one's conscience in spite of the ridicule and torments of one's associates? What does the award to Captain W. say about our nation's official values?

HISTORY: What Does It Teach?

One of America's greatest historians was Charles A. Beard. Damned in his youth for being too radical, in his later years he was condemned for being more conservative than the New Deal culture which he criticized. Still, he made a determined effort to relate history to all of life and civilization, and his ability shone from his many books.

Charles Beard once summed up what history teaches in four sentences:

1. "When it gets dark enough, you can see the stars." The blacker the outlook, the brighter the uplook can be. The greatest periods of history—the most fertile, creative, forward-moving —have been times of chaos, change, revolution, and despair, in the view of many who lived in those periods. The worst times in Jewish history brought forth the greatest prophets—Amos,

Isaiah, Jeremiah. When our lives are the most trying, we can learn the most and rise the highest.

2. "The bee fertilizes the flower that it robs." To every force, President Eisenhower once reminded the nation, there is opposed a counterforce. The barbarians who destroyed the Roman Empire opened the door for Christian culture to spread across Europe and eventually to America. Every dark cloud has a sunny side.

3. "Whom the gods would destroy, they first make mad." A nation's pride and destructive conquests foreshadow its fall. A man who lets himself be controlled by lust or habit or by anything less than God, will succumb to demonic forces.

4. "The mills of the gods grind slowly, but they grind exceeding small." Evil often pays in the short run, but in the long run, time balances the book and righteousness is rewarded. Someday payday arrives. As Abraham Lincoln once reminded the people he served as President, "The judgments of the Lord are true and righteous altogether" (Psalm 19:9).

What else does history teach? Someone once said that history is "His story." Is it? Why? Every day we are making history. What will our grandchildren think when they read about what happened in the last third of the twentieth century? Oliver Wendell Holmes once said, "I find the great thing in this world is not so much where we stand as in what direction we are moving." What is our direction?

HOLY SPIRIT

In his fine book *A Life Full of Surprises* Lloyd John Ogilvie tells of attending a meeting on human relations before which a priest, a Methodist layman, and others talked about the inability of many Christians to do much about the urgent needs of the modern world. The layman said that he had gone to church for years before he had an experience that showed him what Christianity really meant and made his spiritual life vital.

The priest said to him, "My friend, you have received the Holy Spirit!"

What does the Holy Spirit mean to you? It has been said that the Holy Spirit makes Christ real to us, shows us what the Bible means, enables us to pray, and renews the life of God within our hearts and lives. The Spirit appears to be moving and shaking the church throughout the modern world. *Do you know of any examples of this? Is the Holy Spirit a frightening, mysterious being, or a manifestation of God's best in human life?*

For reference: study "Holy Spirit" or "Holy Ghost" in a Bible concordance or index, or a reliable Bible dictionary.

HONESTY: Does It Work in Religion?

Does real honesty work in religion? Keith Miller, one of the most influential Christian laymen alive (for several years his two books *The Taste of New Wine* and *A Second Touch* have led the religious best-seller lists), says he used to tell God he loved him whether he really felt that way or not, because he had been told that is the way a Christian ought to behave. But one morning he felt awful, and instead of the usual hypocrisy he said, "God, I don't like you at all, and I wish you would get off my back." Then . . .

"I lay there in bed waiting for the lightning to strike. But no lightning. So I told him, 'I don't want to feel this way, Lord. I really want to be your person. Help me not to feel this way about Christ.'

"For the first time I had really leveled with God when I did not feel good about him. And a strange thing began to happen in my inner journey. I began to be able to accept all my feelings, which I'd been repressing, and pretending didn't exist, and offer them openly to God for change, shaping and forgiveness. I began to want to find and do his will with a kind of growing excitement. I began to see that the Scriptures are filled with the ruggedness of actual life, but we have sweetened them beyond recognition. Jesus talked about sex, drinking and crooked business deals all the time. Real problems! I began to see that —if we can only sweep away the accumulated sugar—he was talking about the restlessness of modern life."[1]

When we are really honest with God, admitting exactly what and how bad we are, he can begin to do something for us . . . heal us. And when we admit our sins and rottenness to other people, they discover that we are for real, that we are like them . . . and that they can find the divine help we may have been fruitlessly trying to give them.

Does this throw any light on the Pharisee and the Publican in Jesus' parable in Luke (18:9–14)? Here was one man who thought he was just great, spiritually A-1, and another man who could bring to God nothing but an anguished prayer: "God be merciful to me a sinner. . . ."

See also PRAYER: DO WE NEED RULES?; PRAYER: WHAT SHOULD WE PRAY ABOUT?; WORSHIP: CHURCH AND HYPOCRISY.

HOPE: Is Hope Alone Enough?

On the third day of February 1970, Secretary of the Treasury David M. Kennedy made a speech in New York in which he said that the rate of interest, which had been rising for years, might soon drop. Immediately the stock market, which had been drifting downward for many months, jumped upward eleven points. But soon afterward the market dropped to its lowest point in seven years. A few days after Mr. Kennedy's speech the New York *Times* ran this headline:

STOCK RISE ON HOPE ALONE FAILS TO LAST

Hope is important. It can raise spirits as well as stock prices, restore health to the sick, put new zest into the apathetic,

[1] From a speech at the U. S. Congress on Evangelism in Minneapolis, September 1969.

change defeat into victory. But there has to be more than hope alone. Expert analysts said that the stock market lost its February lift because the other factors—the record of decreased profits in many businesses, the increase in unemployment, the decline in sales of a number of products, the business community's uncertainty about what the federal government might do next—did not support economic confidence. So the market slipped and floundered. As soon as these factors changed, many analysts were certain that once again it would bound upward.

Hope should not stand alone. When God encourages us to hope, he reminds us of the other relevant factors: the record of his past performance; the reliability of his promises; the power of his love; the certainty of a great future. There are three great realities that endure: faith, hope and love. The three belong together, and the greatest is love (I Corinthians 13:13).

Exactly what is hope? The renowned Bible scholar Alexander Cruden once defined it as "a firm expectation of all promised good things, so far as they may be for God's glory and our good." Do you agree? Would you say that faith looks up in confidence, and hope looks forward in trust? What does Paul mean when he says, "We are saved by hope" (Romans 8:24)? What can we do to strengthen hope for ourselves? For others?

See also IMMORALITY.

HUNGER AND A NEW FORD

The Ford Motor Company has been experimenting in two Latin American countries with a new two-wheel tractor that sells for about five hundred dollars. Known as the DNT, it helps a farmer produce twice as much as he could with a pair of oxen. Coupling the new tractor with a program of better seeds and fertilizers, the company said it may go far "toward raising the standard of living in the developing nations and reducing the threat of famine in the coming generation."

Wouldn't it be great if this and similar innovations helped

*fill the hungry stomachs of the two thirds of the people in the
world who are perpetually underfed and ill-nourished? This is
an example of private enterprise helping to feed the hungry.
Should it be doing such things? Should our government? Should
church and mission agencies? Or should all three, as is in fact
happening to some extent? To date we have not done enough
to prevent widespread hunger and starvation. What new steps
should be taken?*

HUNGER AND THE GOSPEL

In an article in the October 15, 1969, *United Church
Observer*, Dr. Howard L. Trueman points out that half the
children in the world do not get enough to eat, and that they
contract tuberculosis before they reach the age of fifteen. He says,
". . . if the coming of God's Kingdom on earth is to have any
meaning at all for over half of mankind, it will first be when
they do not have to lie down hungry at night. They have no
concern whatever as to whether God is 'wholly other' or whether
he is 'immanent' within them. I think we have to face the fact
that . . . man is becoming much less concerned about the
destination of his soul in some afterlife than he is about his
security in this one."[1]

*Have you ever been really hungry—without the security of
knowing there was plenty of food close by? Did you know that
about half the world's money, cars, television sets, and other
goodies are in the United States? How much do we love the
people of the world? If we were starving, how interested would
we be in hearing someone talk about God and heaven?*

HUNGER, EDUCATION, SUNDAY SCHOOL

Within the past few years there have been various charges
and countercharges about hunger in America. At first such a

[1] Used by permission.

thing seemed too impossible to believe. Then the evidence began to come in from various parts of the United States. It began to appear that even if few people were actually hungry, a number of children suffered from improper nutrition—and this affected education.

The New York State Education Department reported to New York's Governor Nelson Rockefeller in January 1970, that children who are undernourished cannot be properly educated, and may have problems of comprehension and behavior. Such children, said the investigators, show apathy in school, cannot concentrate on their lessons, often fail to understand, and are apt to be generally retarded in learning. The Governor noted on January 10, "Proper nutrition contributes importantly to raising the level of achievement and social development of all children."

Perhaps it does not make sense spending money trying to educate children in our public schools unless we provide the conditions for learning, through enough food. Otherwise the money for schooling is wasted.

And why spend money on Sunday schools if the children can't learn? Many people want the church to concentrate on religion, but what is closer to religion than making Sunday school effective?

On another level, what about crime and juvenile delinquency? If food can help such problems, doesn't it make sense morally and religiously for the churches to pitch in—as so many are doing—to try to help every child have enough food to grow up properly?

Missionaries in other countries have understood this for many years. In America for a long time we couldn't believe that anyone was actually hungry. Now we are beginning to realize how some of our citizens live, and to help them. *Far from being socialistic, isn't this the only decent thing, the only Christian, democratic thing we can do about a problem that refuses to stay swept under the rug?*

IDEALS AND DEEDS

"The basic complaint that most young people make about their elders is not that their ideals are wrong, but that they do not take them seriously enough.

"'I really can't put my dad down for what he believes,' a student told me a few months back. 'The trouble is he never did anything about it.'"[1]

Is this complaint justified, in terms of the difference between the older and younger generations today? Do we take seriously what we believe? If we really believe something, is it possible not to live according to that belief? What do our lives say about our belief in God, or in the ethics of the Ten Commandments, or in the Christian way of life, or about our loyalty to our church or nation?

IMMORTALITY: An Ancient Hope

In 1908, a human body 50,000 years old was discovered in a cave near La Chapelle-aux-Saints, France. The noted American anthropologist Loren Eiseley commented about the ancient remains in a scientific symposium: "Massive flint-hardened hands had shaped a sepulcher, and placed flat stones to guard the dead man's head. A haunch of meat had been left to aid the dead man's journey. Worked flints, a little treasure of the human dawn, had been poured lovingly into the grave. And down the untold centuries the message had come without words: 'We too were human, we too suffered, we too believed that the grave is not the end. We too, whose faces affright you now, knew human agony and human love.'"

Love and hope are older than some of us realized. Whence comes this worldwide, ancient surmise that this life is not all? An old song begins, "My hope is built on nothing less . . ." What is your hope built on?

See also ETERNITY, DEATH AND RESURRECTION, HOPE.

[1] Harvey Cox in *Think*, copyright © 1969 by IBM.

Look at any economic chart that covers a few decades. Check the dates of the troughs and peaks of business upswings and downswings, and you will note that every war is followed by a wild surge of inflation.

The January 1970 *Dateline,* published by the eminently respectable National Association of Manufacturers, carries an article by William H. Chartener, vice-president-economist of Goldman, Sachs and Company, entitled "What *Not* to Do About Inflation." He writes: "The causes of the inflation we now have are varied and interactive. . . . [But] The war in Vietnam can be identified as the single most important initiating element in our present inflation."

Those who are concerned about the morality (or immorality) of the war in Southeast Asia are not thinking only of what it is doing to that poverty-stricken edge of Asia. They are also thinking of what it is doing to us. Inflation robs those least able to pay: the poor and the aged.

Here is a widow with a tiny Social Security check and an annuity that is supposed to see her through the rest of her life. But every month both checks shrink, in actuality, as the costs of everything skyrocket. What she and her husband saved in good faith has been stolen by the bombs and gases dropped on distant peasants.

War carries an exorbitant price tag. Who can pay back what it is doing to our own citizens in the U.S.A.? Shouldn't we be willing to risk something for peace?

See also PEACE, WAR.

INFORMATION AND FAITH

Meyer Berman is one stockbroker who is happy when the stock market is falling. In 1969 while most people got ulcers over the market's Niagara-like descent, Mr. Berman made money. A confirmed skeptic, he doesn't believe what he hears about a stock's rosy prospects unless he investigates. When he does, he often finds reason to believe it will go down instead of up, and he is right often enough to have a fourteen-room house with a four-car garage.

The Berman method is selling short. Buying a stock on credit and gambling that it will fall, he sells it immediately and pays for it later when its value is much less. But his "gambles" are backed up with hard work. Before buying the stock of one company, noted the *Wall Street Journal,* Berman telephoned a friend in London, the American Embassy in Tokyo, and other knowledgeable people as far away as Jakarta. He puts most of his waking hours into his work. And while other people are guessing or hoping, Meyer Berman has the facts to back up his moves.

Religion can be too intellectual, but it runs the risk of getting its head so high in the clouds that its feet lose contact with the real world. Jesus took the Old Testament commandment, "You shall love the Lord your God with all your heart, and with all your soul, and with all your might" (Deuteronomy 6:5), and added something new—*"and with all your mind"* (Mark 12:30).

Dr. John Sutherland Bonnell once received this complaint from a member of his congregation: He makes people think too much. "I like a church," said the complainant, "where I can unscrew my head and leave it under the pew until the end of the service." But there is no room in Christianity for unscrewed heads. The challenges of a ruthless, loveless age demand all our brains and all our hearts too.

How well are we informed about these people in our own country: Mexican-Americans? Puerto Ricans? Cubans? Blacks? Migrant farm workers? Inner-city dwellers? Indians? Native Alaskans? What do we know about their problems? About what the churches in many places are doing for such people? About what the government and other groups are doing, and not doing? About their own needs and desires?

How well-informed are we about the principles of our Con-

stitution, and of the Bill of Rights? How much do we know about what Congress, the Administration, and the courts are doing, and why? Does our information come from reliable, accurate sources, or from extremist groups?

How much information do we have about our faith? About the Bible, how it came to us, the facts in it and its central emphases? About Christ and the church? About the two thousand years of Christian struggle since the New Testament ended?

How much do we know about the daily-increasing dangers of the population explosion, water pollution, air pollution, the depletion of our natural resources, the increase in crime and violence and militarism?

How well does information back up and enhance our faith?

INHUMANITY AND MORAL STANDARDS: Any Connection?

How can human beings shoot down women and children in cold blood, torture other human beings to death, do all the inhuman things that seem to characterize the twentieth century? What made the German people accept Hitler and the monstrous crimes of Nazism? In his *History of Modern Germany 1840–1945,* the European historian Hajo Holborn answers the second question with the statement that there was a decline in German education resulting in the graduation of students unprepared for civic responsibility and lacking in "absolute ethical commitments." Holborn adds: "The higher philosophy and humanities of the period were largely formalistic or relativistic and did not provide a firm faith. In these circumstances, it was inevitable that so many people fell for cheap and simple interpretations of life and history, as offered by racists."

Today we are sometimes told that there are no absolutes, that even truth is relative, changeable. Young people are urged to evolve their own philosophies of values. *Is there a connection, as historian Holborn suggests, between such relativism and savagery? Do our young people face life with "a firm faith"? Do we offer them a foundation for civic and social responsibility by our own example? Is it possible to be flexible about the form of faith and still hold to the "absoluteness" of right, truth, love?*

See also COMMANDMENTS AND COURTROOMS, MORALITY.

INTERNATIONAL RELATIONSHIPS

PLAYING HOUSE[1]

The other day I went
Over to Lu Lin's house to play.
She didn't have a single doll
That closed its eyes; not one
That drank out of a bottle.
They were made of colored paper,
With no white face among them.

I told Lu Lin about a wicked Monster
Who had a scheme to kidnap her and her dolls.
When she cried I gave her one of my cookies,
And promised I'd save her from the Monster.

So I found a match
And touched the paper houses
Where she kept her dolls.
At that, her little brother flew at me, screaming,
"Those dolls are ours! You go away!"

But I was bigger than he,
And knew much better how to fight.

[1] Copyright 1968 Christian Century Foundation. Reprinted by permission from the January 17, 1968, issue of *The Christian Century* and by permission of the author.

I burned those trashy huts, each one;
Then I cleaned things up.

When Lu Lin cried for her dolls
I gave her another cookie . . . her brother, too.
They looked all broken up, ungrateful ones!

But I know I did right:
For I saved Lu Lin from the Monster;
And I showed her how to play house—
The right way.

—HARRIET R. BEAN

Does this suggest any present-day parallels? If there is a "right way" in world relationships, is it up to one country to decide what the right way is and force it on another one? What do you think of the statement made by a general, "We'll save this place even if we have to destroy it to do it"? Does Christianity suggest any guidelines for the way one country relates to another?

INTERNATIONAL RELATIONSHIPS: Questions for Americans

"How long will the American people remain content with a foreign-aid program that is being reduced at a time when the poor countries are getting relatively poorer and the rich countries, richer? How long will we depend on foreign aid that is largely military aid? How long will we continue to spend billions for war and its preparations, and be unwilling to spend comparable sums to rebuild the cities and eliminate the slums of the whole world?

"How long will we continue to support patterns of world trade that make futile even the heroic efforts towards development of nations which because they have no capital are dependent on unfair and unstabilized prices of primary products which are their only surplus for the market? How long will the white northern nations take advantage of dark southern nations in unequal economic battle?"[1]

Dr. Blake stated that these are moral questions on the answers to which depend the possibility of true peace, adding, "Too few men anywhere take the power of a righteous God seriously."

Should Christianity affect our international relationships? Is peace possible if these relationships are unfair and unjust? Do we have an obligation toward poorer countries? What would Jesus do if he were our Secretary of State?

For reference: Psalm 33:12; Proverbs 14:34; Isaiah 48:22; 32:17; James 2:1–16; I John 2:9, 10.

See also AMERICA, FOREIGN AID, PEACE, WAR.

JESUS: Still at Large

The poster pictures a bearded, revolutionary-looking figure. It reads:

WANTED:

JESUS CHRIST

Alias: the Messiah, Son of God, King of Kings, Lord of Lords, Prince of Peace, etc.

Notorious Leader of an underground liberation movement

Wanted on the following charges:

Practicing medicine, wine making, and food distribution without a license

Interfering with business in the temple

Associating with known criminals, radicals, subversives, prostitutes, and street people

Claiming to have the power to make people over

Appearance: Typical hippie type—long hair, beard, robe, sandals, etc.

[1] Dr. Eugene Carson Blake in a speech in Washington, D.C., November 14, 1969.

Hangs around slum areas, few rich friends, often sneaks
    out of town into the country

Has a group of disreputable followers sometimes called
    "freemen" (they claim he has set them free)

Beware: This man is extremely dangerous. His insidious,
inflamatory message is particularly dangerous to young
people who haven't been taught to ignore him.

    WARNING: THIS MAN IS STILL AT LARGE!

A furor was set off in several communities when this poster was
reproduced in underground newspapers. Many people were dis-
turbed by the implication that Jesus had anything in common
with hippies or radicals. Yet this poster is distributed by a
Christian group to call attention to the fact that God is not
dead, that Jesus is at large in the world today.

*Do you believe that? Is Jesus a living person to you? How
do you think he would be treated now if he had been born
in 1940 A.D. instead of 4 B.C.? What do you think he would
do in modern America? One student said, "We don't like the
church, but we love Jesus." Are we ever guilty of putting
the church ahead of Christ?*

JUSTICE: Doing It

A man named James Earl Ray is subject to life imprisonment
for the murder of Martin Luther King, Jr. Before Ray was
sentenced, many people expected him to be executed for the
murder and many others doubted that he was the sole as-
sassin. James Bevel—a member of the staff of the Southern
Christian Leadership Conference which King had led—expressed his feelings about those who came to Memphis for a
memorial service for Dr. King:

"I think I can prove in a court that Ray did not kill
Martin King. But even if Ray did it, we are still going the
wrong way. How can we Christians think that we are *doing*
justice by killing another man? . . .

"Here, once again, you had these people . . . moaning over a dead man, when Jesus himself said very plainly to us: 'Let the dead bury the dead!' There was a man, very much alive and very much in trouble [Ray], sitting right there in that jail in Memphis, and *not one of them asked to go visit him. . . .*

"I told them that if you wanted to march and hold lighted candles, you ought to march and hold candles in support of James Earl Ray, and help him to have a just trial."[1]

How are we to "do justice"? Can a man have a fair trial when he is tried and convicted in advance by government officials and by the news media? Does it serve the cause of justice to take one life for the taking of another?

JUSTICE: For Everyone?

Lee Berry is an epileptic. Early in 1969 he was in the hospital when he heard that the police were looking for him. Mr. Berry telephoned the police and told them where he was. They came to the hospital, removed Mr. Berry from his bed, handcuffed him, and imprisoned him in New York City's Tombs.

There, according to Mrs. Lee Berry, he was denied the medication he needed (he had suffered an epileptic seizure several weeks earlier and had been hospitalized for it when he was arrested), beaten, and held for months. Finally he was transferred to Bellevue Hospital.

When Mr. and Mrs. Leonard Bernstein and other prominent New Yorkers heard what had been done to Mr. Berry, they sought legal help for the imprisoned epileptic. The fact that he is a Black Panther did not lessen their desire for justice.

Does everyone deserve justice, or only people who belong to the "right" organizations? If the Constitution does not apply to everyone, can we expect it to apply to us? Does God love only "good" people? It is not popular to befriend someone

[1] In *Katallagete*, Winter 1968–69.

connected with an organization considered dangerous or subversive. Does that lessen our responsibility for treating the members legally and fairly?

Nearly four hundred years ago the English poet-clergyman John Donne wrote: "No man is an island, entire of itself; every man is a piece of the continent, a part of the main; if a clod be washed away by the sea, Europe is the less, as well as if a promontory were, as well as if a manor of thy friends or of thine own were; any man's death diminishes me, because I am involved in mankind; and therefore never send to know for whom the bell tolls; it tolls for thee."

Yes, we are all a part of mankind. Any man's degradation diminishes me. When the rights of anyone are endangered, the rights of none are safe.

John Donne was involved in mankind. Jesus Christ was involved in mankind. Are we?

JUSTICE AND CHARITY

"I would like to see less emphasis on so-called charity and more emphasis on justice: I would like to see fewer Christmas hampers and bales of old clothes and more action to correct the conditions that make hampers and the gifts of used clothing necessary."[1]

If you were out of work, would you rather have a Christmas turkey or a job? What does it mean to love your neighbor as yourself? If we as a society treat anyone with less than equality and justice, is any amount of charity for that person enough? Christians have long supported welfare projects, trying to care for people who are down and out. Do Christians have a right to try to repair the machinery of society so that there are fewer dropouts? When the church began, individuals could do nothing in their totalitarian monarchy. What would Jesus and Paul and Peter be doing if they were on earth today?

[1] Rev. A. C. Forrest, editor of Canada's *United Church Observer,* in the *Western Catholic Reporter,* December 28, 1969.

LAW AND CONSCIENCE: The Convict Buried at Wheaton College

"Just north of Williston hall and the dining hall is the grave of James E. Burr, abolitionist and friend of Wheaton's first president, Dr. Jonathan Blanchard.

"Marked by a flat headstone, the inscription reads: 'James E. Burr, Died April 26, 1859. Age 45. Here Lies the Friend of the Oppressed, Who Became a Martyr for the Right.'

"According to *Prison Life and Reflection,* a book written by George Thompson, Thompson, Burr and Alanson Work served a period of imprisonment in the Missouri State Penitentiary. They were arrested on July 12, 1841, for assisting some slaves to cross the Mississippi River near Palmyra, Missouri, into the free state of Illinois. . . . They were enroute to a preaching engagement when they were arrested. . . . Burr . . . married and became a trustee and member of the Congregational Church."[1]

There were professing Christians in the America of a hundred years ago who did not question whether there were laws higher than the laws of the state, who did not believe that Christians could live apart from the social problems around them, who were willing to break laws and go to jail if necessary to do the will of God as they saw it, who did not believe that the law of the land was necessarily the law of God, who knew that there might be a difference between the two and were prepared to incur the wrath of the state when their consciences told them to defy it.

"In 1928," the *Record* article continues, "the college board of trustees, for reasons not clear, authorized the removal of the body and monument to a nearby Wheaton cemetery."

"Did you know a convict was buried on the campus of Wheaton?" I asked a recent graduate of the college.

"No, I never heard of that."

In the nineteenth century there were men and women who knew that black is beautiful, that color is no ground for con-

[1] Jan Cooper in *The Wheaton Record,* April 30, 1959.

demnation, that all men are created by God. In the nineteenth century there were preachers who broke the laws and went to jail. There were Christians who honored them—as Wheaton's President Blanchard honored James E. Burr and insisted that he be buried on the campus—and there were other professing Christians who found all sorts of reasons in the Bible for an entirely different line of reasoning.

Sounds like today, doesn't it?

At the end of his Sermon on the Mount, Jesus talked about the difference between talking and doing something (Matthew 7:15–27). Could that have any bearing on this?

LIFE ON EARTH: How Long Will It Last?

No birds sing in Tonto National Forest, Arizona. Few animals are born, and many of these are deformed. People living nearby are losing weight, suffering chest pains and internal hemorrhaging and other effects of herbicide poisoning.

The herbicides have been sprayed from airplanes onto the Tonto Forest since 1965 in a forest-ranger program to increase water runoff by killing trees. The spray has been very effective as a killer; even fruit trees near the forest are now fruitless.

The herbicides, according to a news special by Steven V. Roberts in the February 8, 1970, New York *Times,* are 2-4-5-T, 2-4D and Silvex, and tests of these chemicals recently have shown that they are dangerous to human and animal, as well as vegetable, life. The American Cancer Society has found that more than two thirds of the babies born to white mice exposed to 2-4-5-T are born deformed.

Robert McKusick, whose property is nearly surrounded by the Tonto National Forest, and whose goats are now born dead or deformed more often than not, says, "The real danger is not to us or our animals but to the environment. If they try to spray again, we'll shoot them down."

Meanwhile, according to the February 7, 1970, *New Yorker,* for seven years America has been spraying 2-4-5-T and other deadly defoliants on South Vietnam, "on the countryside, on villages, and on South Vietnamese men and women in staggering amounts. . . . Since 1962, the defoliation operations have covered almost five million acres, an area equivalent to about 12 percent of the entire territory of South Vietnam, and about the size of the state of Massachusetts."

This *New Yorker* article by Thomas Whiteside points out that the United States has set up guidelines for the amount of 2-4-5-T permissible in American drinking water. Vietnamese citizens must drink water containing 2-4-5-T "at six hundred times the concentration officially considered safe for Americans."

In *The Progressive* for November, 1969, Senator Gaylord A. Nelson wrote: "Man, ironically, may be the creature that left as his monument a planet nearly as incapable of sustaining life as its barren neighbors in the dead vacuum of the solar system we are now exploring at costs that are fantastically greater than we are prepared to spend to preserve our own planet."

How much longer will man be able to go on tinkering with things he does not understand, or prefers to ignore, as he kills, deforms, and destroys life on earth? In our American democracy, we are the persons ultimately responsible for all this. How many citizens realize what we are doing to ourselves and to the envelope of life in which we maintain a precarious existence? How long can we continue before the situation is, as the scientists phrase it, irreversible? How much poison will our air, our water, and our plants and animals tolerate before there is no water fit to drink, no food fit to eat, no air we can breathe?

LISTENING

"God has listened to you enough times," says an advertisement from *Religion in American Life.* "Now how about listening to him?"

What is God saying? "Listen," says the ad. " 'Love your

neighbor as yourself.' If that were put to practice—really to practice—ghettos would not exist, wars would cease, hunger would end. . . . One thing is certain, we won't even *begin* to see it, if we don't start *doing* what God has asked of us for heaven only knows how long."

A good many million words must have been addressed to God over the years. How many of his words have been heard? Dr. Ralph Sockman once said that one great difference between our forefathers and ourselves is that they began the day with the Bible and prayer, while we begin it with the morning newspaper. Some of us think it's important to read both the newspaper and the Bible. What would happen if we gave God equal time? If we listened to what he has to tell us, and then did it?

LOVE IN PRACTICE: "A Man Going From Atlanta . . ."

Have you ever read this about Jesus?

"One day a teacher of an adult Bible class got up and tested him with this question: 'Doctor, what does one do to be saved?'

"Jesus replied, 'What does the Bible say? How do you interpret it?'

"The teacher answered, 'Love the Lord your God with all your heart and with all your soul and with all your physical strength and with all your mind; and love your neighbor as yourself.'

" 'That is correct,' answered Jesus. 'Make a habit of this and you'll be saved.'

"But the Sunday-school teacher, trying to save face, asked, 'But . . . er . . . but . . . just who *is* my neighbor?'

"Then Jesus laid into him and said, 'A man was going from Atlanta to Albany and some gangsters held him up. When they had robbed him of his wallet and brand-new suit, they beat him up and drove off in his car, leaving him unconscious on the shoulder of the highway.

132

" 'Now it just so happened that a white preacher was going down that same highway. When he saw the fellow, he stepped on the gas and went scooting by.[1]

" 'Shortly afterwards a white gospel-song leader came down the road, and when he saw what had happened, he too stepped on the gas.[2]

" 'Then a black man traveling that way came upon the fellow, and what he saw moved him to tears. He stopped and bound up his wounds as best he could, drew some water from his water jug to wipe away the blood, and then laid him on the back seat.[3] He drove on into Albany and took him to the hospital and said to the nurse, "You all take good care of this white man I found on the highway. Here's the only two dollars I got, but you all keep account of what he owes, and if he can't pay for it, I'll settle up with you when I make a payday." '

" 'Now if you had been the man held up by the gangsters, which of these three—the white preacher, the white song leader, or the black man—would you consider to have been your neighbor?'

"The teacher of the adult Bible class said, 'Why of course, the nig—I mean, er . . . well, er . . . the one who treated me kindly.'

"Jesus said, 'Well, then, *you* get going and start living like that!' "

[1] "His homiletical mind probably made the following outline: (a) I do not know the man. (b) I do not wish to get involved in any court proceedings. (c) I don't want to get blood on my new upholstery. (d) The man's lack of proper clothing would embarrass me upon my arrival in town. (e) And finally, brethren, a minister must never be late for worship services.

[2] "What his thoughts were we'll never know, but as he whizzed past, he may have been whistling, 'Brighten the corner, where you are.'

[3] "All the while his thoughts may have been along this line: 'Somebody's robbed you; yeah, I know about that. I been robbed, too. And they done beat you up bad: I know, I been beat up, too. And everybody just go right on by and leave you laying here hurting. Yeah, I know. They pass me by, too.' "

The above is Luke 10:25–37 as translated by Clarence Jordan in his inimitable book *The Cotton Patch Version of Luke and Acts.*[4] Check your own translation and see what you think the point of Jesus' story was.

We seldom pick up hitchhikers today; we are warned against the dangers. Were there dangers, do you suppose, for the man who stopped to pick up the fellow who had fallen among thieves, in the days before there were state police? We often discuss what love is, or means. Is there any better example than Jesus' illustration?

Clarence Jordan lived the way he talked and wrote. He put on no airs; he had a doctor's degree, but spent his life helping the poor and the dispossessed in Georgia. Denounced as a Communist (he was simply a Christian), shot at, harassed by people who tried to stop what he was doing, Clarence Jordan seemed to many of us more like Jesus Christ than most of the people we found in the twentieth century. His whole life was love in action.

What is our life?

LOVE IN WARTIME: Does It Pay Off?

Those who consider themselves "realists" are inclined to say that such things as love and peace are "beautiful ideals" but that they are not practical—especially against national enemies.

Sergeant Vernon C. Shepard of Akron, Ohio, was in an American helicopter that was shot down by guerrillas of North Vietnam. When he was released, Sergeant Shepard testified, "I was never tortured. I was humanely treated. These people took the best care of us they could as far as medicine and food; we got primarily the same thing as they did."

The result? "I could never take arms against these people, the way they treated me," said the sergeant. "That will be my view forever."

[4] Association Press, copyright © 1969 by Clarence Jordan. Used by permission.

Love and decency got rid of an enemy the best way: by changing him into a friend. Sergeant Shepard's buddy, Michael T. Peterson of Redmond, Washington, felt the same way: "I can't say I agree with their political views and what not. [But] I really don't feel I could go to war against them again. . . ." How many others have been changed no one knows, and no one can say that what is right pays off immediately and visibly. But treating someone as we would like to be treated does provide a highly viable alternative to the dead end of contempt, torture, inhumanity, murder. For sooner or later, what we sow, we reap.

Is love a practical attitude? Is hate? Does love between individuals or nations exclude possible discipline of some kind, or judgment, or reasonable defenses? Does it sometimes require these? Are all wars just? If not, what should our attitude be toward those who believe in selective conscientious objection— the view that one cannot fight in a particular war because he is convinced that that particular war is wrong? Could you burn alive people who had shared their food and medicine with you?

LUCK, OR A DIVINE PLAN? The Hobbit

One of the most popular authors with young people today is J. R. R. Tolkien, author of *The Hobbit* and *The Lord of the Rings*. "The hobbit" is a furry little creature named Bilbo who is persuaded by the wizard Gandalf to go on a long journey with some dwarfs to recover a horde of treasure from a fire-breathing dragon. After many narrow escapes, the dragon is killed and the treasure is won back, and the people of that place make songs saying that the rivers run with gold—just as the old songs had prophesied.

"Then the prophecies of the old songs have turned out to be true, after a fashion!" says Bilbo.

"Of course!" says Gandalf. "And why should not they prove true? Surely you don't disbelieve the prophecies, because you had a hand in bringing them about yourself? You don't really suppose, do you, that all your adventures and escapes were managed by mere luck, just for your sole benefit?"

Tolkien is a Christian and was a friend of the late C. S. Lewis; although Tolkien insists that there are no hidden allegories in his stories, they are full of hints and surmises pointing to abiding truths.

Does luck govern the world, or is a divine plan slowly unfolding? In other ages it may have been easier than now to believe that God was on the throne, everything slowly progressing toward a foreordained, beneficent end. Today, with chaos everywhere, a number of our best leaders dead, small men in high places, and the things we counted on most (like science) getting out of control, it may be easier to believe with the atheists that luck or fate is the ultimate reality. *But is it?*

Is it possible the ancient prophecies are right, after all? Would they be less true if we had to help carry them out by our own hardest efforts? Do we need a higher perspective to appreciate the purpose of creation? Why on earth are we here? For heaven's sake?

MAJORITIES AND MINORITIES

When more people than ever before in history gathered in Washington, D.C., on November 14 and 15 to express their concern over United States foreign policy, and millions more expressed similar concern throughout the nation, the statement was made that these citizens were only an irresponsible minority and that a "silent majority" held no such desire for peace and international justice. At the Washington gathering, Senator George McGovern, who is also an active Methodist layman, said:

"We meet today because we love America. We love America enough to call her to a higher standard. We love America enough to call her away from the folly of war to the blessings of peace. . . .

"We do not make guesses about what the silent majority

may be thinking, rather we heed the words of Emerson: 'If a single man plant himself on his instincts and there abide, the huge world will come round to him.' . . .

"We say to those who would divide Americans against Americans by appeals to ignorance, passion and fear—'You do your worst, and we will do our best.'

"So let me close on that timeless admonition: 'Be strong and of good courage; be not afraid; neither be thou dismayed.' . . ."[1]

Which is better: to do what you think everyone else is doing or likes—or to do what you believe is right? Were Christ's disciples a majority or a minority? Does the truth depend on how many people think it is true? Can a majority repeal the law of gravity? The moral law? The fact that two plus three equal five?

A newspaper reader thought about majorities and minorities and wrote a letter to the editor. The *Record* published it on January 9, 1970:

"There is a silent majority! They remain silent while our air becomes putrid, while the military contracts run $20 billions over cost, while the Ku Klux Klan swears it will do deadly battle with Negroes, silent while Americans rob the nation of taxes by using numbered accounts in Swiss banks, silent when it is announced that senators, judges and public officials are friends of the Mafia and the interest lobbies, silent while the ghettos rot, silent when it is charged that American soldiers brutalize women and children in Vietnam. Yes, there is a silent majority. They are a stupid, indifferent, smug, philistine, complacent, sheepish, greedy majority. . . .

M. Paulson

918 Maple Avenue
Fair Lawn, New Jersey, Dec. 9, 1969"[2]

Strong words! Yet how often majority opinion has had to yield to the astronomical discoveries of one Galileo, the moral

[1] Used by permission of Senator McGovern.
[2] Used by permission of the *Record*.

outrage of one Martin Luther, the religious insight of one St. Paul, the wisdom of one Socrates, the vision of one Amos or Isaiah . . .

MAN: Come of Age?

"There's been a fashionable theological outlook which is a sort of respectable second cousin to the God-is-dead frolic and which says that man has come of age, he's on his own. God has released us to ourselves and he isn't there to help us, to guide and direct us anymore. He has brought us to maturity. We know what we have to do now; all we have to do is do it.

"I suspect that people who think like this never liked being told what to do anyway. Or maybe they couldn't get the hang of how to listen, or couldn't sit still long enough, or had too much to say themselves, so they just took the silence to mean that God was over and out.

"Or maybe they're afraid of their dependency needs. Afraid if they listen they'll also lean. Go soft and helpless. Won't stand on their own two feet.

"How anybody who's had even the most rudimentary run-in with God can walk off with that idea is beyond me. If there's anything God won't do, it's anything you're able to do yourself. But if you let him, he'll throw a little light on the matter; he might even show you how to do it better.

"But of course that means working harder, so if you'd rather not bother just tell the old dad you don't need him anymore. Tell him to keep his bright ideas to himself; tell him you're all grown up now; you're on your own.

"I have a hunch you will be."

—Emily A. Swinnerton[1]

As we understand some theological experts, they seem to be saying what Emily A. Swinnerton says they are trying to tell us:

[1] Used by permission of the author.

We're on our own, ready to get along without God. If they don't mean that, they should make clear what they do mean. But if that is what they do mean, we have to agree with Mrs. Swinnerton.

What man or woman is more noble and fully human than when he falls to his knees, as Lincoln sometimes did, asking God's help in the struggle against evil?

MANHOOD: Bucking the System

Sven Eriksson is a young veteran of the war in Vietnam who lives in fear. While on a reconnaissance mission, Sven's buddies kidnapped a pretty teen-age Vietnamese girl, planning to have some "fun" for a few days and then dispose of the evidence—her. When Sven refused to join the fun, the others questioned his manhood. After she had been brutally raped and killed, Sven told the army authorities, thinking the triple crime would be quickly punished. It wasn't. Instead, Sven was advised to keep quiet, not to buck the system. He narrowly escaped being killed. Many of his companions condemned him for seeking justice.

But Sven persisted, and finally the men involved were given sentences which were progressively reduced or canceled. When the two men who stabbed and shot the girl get out of prison, Sven knows that they may well kill him and his family for revenge. Why didn't he go along with the "silent majority"? Why did he buck the system?

Sven lives with fear, Daniel Lang intimates in his book about Sven's experience in Vietnam, *Casualties of War*. But he also lives in the peace of having done something he knew he should, in the integrity of his own convictions, in the clear conscience of not joining in a horrible crime. He is a bigger and better man than some of his military buddies.

What is manhood? Acting worse than an animal? Or living like a man who respects individuals and their rights? What

makes a man stand up and say, as Martin Luther once did,
"Here I stand. I can do no other."

MANKIND: Catastrophe Ahead, or Hope?

Claude Lévi-Strauss is a French anthropologist who is not optimistic about the future of man. In an interview with John L. Hess in the New York *Times,* December 31, 1969, he likened the human situation to a bag of flour full of maggots. "When the population of these worms increases," he said, "even before they meet, before they become conscious of one another, they secrete certain toxins that kill at a distance—that is, they poison the flour they are in, and they die. I think what's happening on the human scale is a little the same sort of thing. We are secreting psychological and moral toxins."

To think that our pollution of the air and water, even our erosion of the moral atmosphere with crime and pornography, might be an unconscious response to overpopulation by poisoning ourselves, is a chilling thought. Yet in this age of destruction and danger, we ought to listen carefully to those who may see us more realistically than we can see ourselves. Still, even an admittedly gloomy specialist in the affairs of man such as anthropologist Lévi-Strauss is not without any hope at all. While he sees the 1970s as a tragic decade of increasing "pollution of the air, the pollution of the water, the destruction of living species one after the other," he believes the trend toward man-made catastrophe could be reversed. How?

"It would take a spiritual revolution as great as that which led to the advent of Christianity," he told John Hess. "It would require that man, who since the Renaissance has been brought up to adore himself, acquire modesty, and that he learn the lesson of all the atrocities we have experienced for thirty or forty years."

A spiritual revolution . . . isn't that what Christianity wants, too, and hopes for? Our faith turned the world upside down once. What if we let its force loose again? If there is a spiritual revival, will it come in time to save us from catastrophe?

It's interesting that a scientist connects the great Renaissance, when learning flowered and modern science was born, with the beginning of a dangerous self-adoration in man. Christianity has always taught that the greatest peril is pride; the supreme need, humility and dependence on God. *Is this the way modern man is to "learn modesty"?*

In 1969 a group of young men and women in long robes and sandals carried homemade crosses to Times Square in New York and stood among the crowds as an ominous warning. They had come from California, they said, to tell this nation that the end is near unless we repent and turn back to God. Perhaps they were right in more ways than anyone realized.

MARRIAGE: Priorities for Happiness

"A written priority list might be helpful to you in attaining or preserving a happy marriage. Begin by making a list of the things you want. Be sure to list the trivial along with the vital things. Put the items down just any old way at first. Your list might look like this:

THINGS I'D LIKE TO HAVE

    my own way
    a mink coat
    a happy marriage
    no ashes on the rug
    a vacation at the beach
    hollandaise sauce on the asparagus
    sheets tucked in at the foot of the bed

"Then after you've made your list—and it might go on for pages—recopy it, putting the most important item at the top, the next most important second and so on down to the thing you care least about.

"You'll recognize right away that some of the items are

incompatible. Your husband can't stand sheets tucked in at the foot of the bed. So which do you want most—a happy marriage or tucked-in sheets? You can't have them both."

—Irene Harrell[1]

Do you know any families that would be happier if both husband and wife did that?

MATURITY: "I'M OK—You're OK"

In his book *I'm OK—You're OK,* Dr. Thomas A. Harris says that there are four basic attitudes toward life. The newborn infant feels helpless in relation to his all-powerful parents, dispensers of food, warmth and happiness, and soon gets the idea, "I'm not OK—you're OK." He either retains this outlook or acquires another. When he realizes his parents' "fallibility" he may think either, "I'm not OK—you're not OK" (an attitude of hopelessness—the individual is worthless and so is everyone else), or "I'm OK—you're not OK" (a psychotically criminal conclusion—the attitude that only the individual is right).

The mature adult, says Dr. Harris, grows into the attitude that both he and others are basically worthwhile. "I'm OK—you're OK."

What is maturity? The New Testament says a number of things about growing. What did Jesus say about spiritual growth? What did the Apostles say?

For reference: Mark 4:28, 30–32; Ephesians 4:14, 15; II Thessalonians 1:3; II Peter 3:18.

See also GROWTH.

MISTAKES: Good for What?

"I don't like these cold, precise, perfect people who, in order not to speak wrong, never speak at all, and in order not to do wrong, never do anything."

[1] In *Good Marriages Grow* (Word Books). Used by permission.

So said Henry Ward Beecher, famous pastor of a Congregational church in Brooklyn during the Civil War.

Jesus said, "Be ye therefore perfect" (Matthew 5:48). Does that mean doing nothing so we won't make mistakes? Our Lord himself exemplified the very opposite of this. While certain religious leaders criticized him for not imitating *their* negative "goodness," he risked being accused of working on the Sabbath by healing people on the holy day and of being a drunkard and glutton by associating with ordinary people who probably did at times eat and drink too much. That part of the Sermon on the Mount where Jesus talks about being perfect is illuminating. Beginning at verse 43, he emphasizes love—the love of God, who sends his sunshine and his refreshing rain down on good and evil alike. The Saviour says in effect, "You must be like him—not just being civil to civil people, but showing the love of God to the unlovely, the sinful, the criminals, and the haters."

Which is better: never drinking or smoking, or concentrating on doing positive things even at the risk of being criticized? Are we responsible for keeping the slate of life free from mistakes—or for taking the risk of getting involved and living in the kind of love Jesus talked about?

MONEY: Earn 7½ Percent Interest!

"Blowup Bank," said the newspaper advertisement, "offers you the highest interest rates in today's money market." The rates followed: 7½ percent, 7 percent, 6¾ percent, 6½ percent, 6¼ percent, 6 percent, 5¾ percent.

Having managed to put a few hundred dollars in a savings bank at the best rate I could find—5 percent interest—I read on with interest. Then I came to the catch, in small type: "Deposits of $100,000 or more." Not having $1000, let alone $100,000, I turned the page.

But I thought about it later. If I had a few hundred thousands of dollars instead of a few hundred, I could hardly help making money at fantastic rates. The more one has, apparently, the more he gets, and vice versa. No wonder we are told the gap between the rich and the poor in this country is steadily enlarging. Hit with inflation, the poor find their dollars steadily shrinking, while the same inflation puts more money than ever into the pockets of those who need it least.

Justice is one of the primary fundamentals of Judaism, Christianity, and every religion worth the name. Is our economy just when it soaks the poor to fatten the wealthy? No doubt it's all very clear to financiers and economists, but to the ordinary person something looks fishy when the more someone owns, the more he is given. Should our faith do something about this situation?

See also JUSTICE.

MONEY AND ETHICS: "Only One Thing"

In the near future, leaded gasoline, used so extensively for many years, will probably be a thing of the past. Reports issued early in 1970 indicated its part in polluting the air and injuring people's health. But it may not go without a fight. When the reports on lead were made public, the chairman of one large gasoline corporation issued a typical statement. He said there was no proof of the charges against leaded gasoline, that gasoline without lead would probably produce even worse smog than before—and that eliminating the lead would cost money. Three and a half billion dollars, he estimated: This is what it would cost the motorists, he said. Companies have a way of passing on their costs to their customers.

By now a good many people feel the proof is in—the case against lead is air-tight. But the battle is not over. Robert W. Irvin wrote in the February 9, 1970, Washington *Post* of Ralph Nader's appeal to Wall Street to do something about lead in gasoline. He told more than two thousand money managers that they owed something to the world, that they ought to join the campaign to help get rid of lead. Many who heard Nader speak agree with him, wrote Irvin, but they are too busy making money grow to worry about such things as the smog outside their windows. "The money managers are interested in only one thing—profits. . . . The trouble is that nobody has yet come up with a way to make social betterment profitable."

Has it come to this? Is Robert Irvin correct in saying that managers of money have no interest in anything vitally affecting everyone's health and life? From the way the tobacco interests have fought the statistics about the relationship of tobacco and cancer, from the way the automobile manufacturers have tried to eliminate Ralph Nader instead of trying to correct the defects he pointed out, from the way money talks so loud and clear, one is forced to admit that it may be true.

If so, it is a shocking commentary on present-day life. *If those in positions of power will put profits above human life and safety, what can the young and the unpowerful do but protest? If our society has no way to put money in its place, what can Christians do but try to remold society into a less brutal structure?*

Abraham Lincoln once explained the power of slavery by asking a visitor to put a coin over his eye. As a coin can blot out the light and seem larger than the sun, Lincoln said, money can change a man's perspective.

What are the things you would not do for a million dollars? How many lies are told, promises broken, lives destroyed because money (which is fine in its proper place) creates an inhumane perspective?

MORAL GUIDELINES FOR TOMORROW

Soon, scientists believe, they will be able to reproduce identical individuals like new Fords off an assembly line—a thousand Mia Farrows, a million Cassius Clays, a billion morons for mindless occupations. They are already producing weapons of unbelievable killing power, and every other day someone seems to invent a new way to destroy all life on earth.

Where are the moral and spiritual guidelines for this Frankenstein future that is already on our doorstep? In September 1969 scientists and Nobel Prize winners came from all parts of the world to Stockholm, Sweden, on a five-day search for "The Place of Value in a World of Facts." One of the leading speakers was French Nobel laureate Jacques Monod, who said that our present society is "rocking along with a value system inherited from the eighteenth century, to which we give lip service but in which no one really believes." He added that none of the philosophies and religions and ethical systems that have sustained society in the past are valid in the light of modern scientific knowledge.

What are the Christian guidelines for population control, weapons systems, the automated world of the future? How would you refute Monod's implication that Christianity has had its day? What should Christians be doing about these concerns?

MORALITY: Affirmations

For You Departed is the wonderfully loving tribute of Alan Paton to his dead wife. In it he pays tribute to her wholesomeness of life, "to a morality concerned with affirmations, not prohibitions."

Most of the Old Testament commandments are prohibitions, "Thou shalt nots." Jesus said the two greatest Commandments are these: "Thou shalt love the Lord thy God with all thy heart and soul and strength and mind," and "Thou shalt love thy neighbor as thyself."

Should we concentrate in our personal lives on prohibitions or affirmations? Which is more truly demanding: to avoid doing certain things, or to try to do everything that brings love into our relationships? When we pray, should we emphasize our problems, or the love and power and grace of God to do more than we can ask or think?

MORALITY TODAY

Early in 1970 the news leaked out: The government of France had made an arrangement to sell 100 warplanes to the government of Libya. Because this might increase the friction between Israel and her Arab neighbors, there was a sense of outrage throughout France; as John L. Hess put it in the New York *Times* of January 23, "The feeling of having been deceived was as evident as concern about what was widely assailed as a cynical policy, putting oil and trade above peace and morality."

Just when we think the world is in a hopeless condition, a sense of morality, of the rightness or wrongness of something, crops up somewhere. The world condemned the ruthless moves of Soviet Russia against Hungary's freedom fighters in the 1950s and against Czechoslovakia in the late 1960s. The world rightly or wrongly questions the actions of the United States in Southeast Asia, because the people of most nations believe this, too, is an unwarranted invasion of other people's rights.

Morality is not in the pocket of any one group. In his letter to the Roman Christians, St. Paul said that while the Jewish people have the law of God, the Gentiles too have his law—"what the law requires is written on their hearts, while their conscience also bears witness" (Romans 2:15).

Should we be concerned about what our government does? Is the sale of munitions a concern of religion? Is morality increasing or decreasing—or is this possible to determine?

See also SITUATION ETHICS AND THE GENERATION GAP.

NEW LOOK IN RELIGION: Jesus at Work[1]

"A new-time religion is breaking out," says Rev. Robert Raines, one of the ministers of the First Methodist Church

[1] The following excerpt is reprinted by special permission of *Ladies' Home Journal,* © 1969, Downe Publishing, Inc.

of Germantown, Philadelphia. In the December 1969 issue of *Ladies' Home Journal* he says there's a new breed of Christians whose faith touches emotions but is also marked by intellectual inquiry and social involvement. "They are taking the wraps off a gentle Jesus meek and mild, smelling flowers or carrying lambs, to discover a tough young man who associated with the poor and outcasts of his day, flayed the religious establishment for its hypocrisy and injustice, broke sacred religious laws again and again in order to serve human need, and put on a smashing one-man demonstration in the most influential cathedral of the nation to protest its exploitation of the faithful.

"Jesus can't be put in stained glass anymore. He isn't dead, but alive and well, stirring things up on the streets and in the churches. He's bringing in, not the sheaves, but the revolution of human freedom and justice. He's controversial, as will be congregations that take him seriously."

What will such a faith and such a Christ do for (or to) the church? If such a religious life-style were to take over, says Minister Raines, this would happen:

"1. Young people who are seeking authentic community, meaning, justice, truth, but are now turned off by the hypocrisy and irrelevance of the church, would try out the church again.

"2. The institutional church would shrink radically. There would be fewer church buildings, bureaucrats, congregations, members, clergymen, and dollars. In their place would come new lay ministries and small congregations gathering in homes around issues of common concern.

"3. Christianity would present a life-style that confronts the prevailing culture rather than, as is the case now, conforms to it—with the result that both the cost and joy of being a Christian would be considerably magnified.

"4. The Church would be free to swing into the '70s as a community of searching celebrators with an openness, courage, honesty, compassion and joy which it hasn't had since the first century."

How do you react to Bob Raines's picture of Jesus? Is

his view or the more traditional one closer to the real Man of Galilee?

Do you agree with Raines's analysis of present-day young people? And of the church of the future? Throughout recent years there has been a steady trend in the direction he foresees—shrinking church budgets, dwindling membership lists, fewer "bureaucracies" in the denominations, a general retreat of some kind. But would this really be a retreat if it meant less members but more committed ones—a church smaller but stronger, slimmer, trimmed for action?

What about point 3? If it cost more to be a Christian, would there be more actual joy in it? Is present-day Christianity too easy? What can your church or group be doing about all this?

NUCLEAR DESTRUCTION AND THE BIBLE

Early in 1969, Dr. George Wald, Higgins Professor of Biology at Harvard University, a Nobel Prize winner, startled the world with a fiery, impassioned speech entitled "A Generation in Search of a Future." In it he pleaded for life and for progress, to the delight of countless young people and of all people looking for hope and light in a dark time.

Late the same year, Dr. Wald again startled a great many listeners. In a speech at Southern Colorado State College he said, "the only way the world is going to stop short of the brink of nuclear holocaust is a return to God and the principles of the Bible—and that is what the young people, even the militants, are trying to tell us." He added, "I know that this is the sheerest, non-academic sentimentality, but I'm convinced that this is the only way we are going to prevent the total chaos that we are headed for—and probably within the next ten years."

What do you think Dr. Wald meant? What can we do about it?

What did Moses mean when he said, "I have set before

you life and death, blessing and curse; therefore choose life, that you and your descendants may live" (Deuteronomy 30:19)? (Compare vss. 15–20.) What did Jesus mean when he said there are just two kinds of response to him (Matthew 7:24–27)? Why did he emphasize hearing and doing?

OLDER PEOPLE: Do We Care?

Marie Caillet worked for forty years as a nurse and a worker in various medical institutions. But unlike the physicians and union members who retire on comfortable pensions, Miss Caillet has financial problems. When her doctor gave her a magazine subscription, she couldn't help thinking how much more she needed the money for other things.

She added together the items that constituted her income. Old Age Assistance gave her $89 a month. Her state legislature had voted a $15 increase, but there were no funds in the state treasury, it was said, to grant this increase. A nephew sent her $15 every other month. That was all. Less than $97 a month had to cover housing, food, clothing, and all the other things that cost money—like prescribed drugs, for which the welfare department no longer pays.

Miss Caillet sat down and wrote the magazine a letter. She stated honestly how much she liked the magazine, but added, "I need the money more, even though it is only a few dollars. I'm afraid my doctor, who is so generous, finds it difficult to understand how such a person as myself gets along; the affluent seldom are able to. But I'm sure you understand, and I would be grateful if you could send me the amount of the subscription. Perhaps I should be ashamed to make a request like this, but I am not. I am poor only in money."

(The editors not only returned to Miss Caillet the amount that had been sent, but gave her a complimentary subscription.)

We speak of "respect for age." What kind of respect do we as a society show for old age when we permit individuals *like Miss Caillet, who have given lifetimes of service to others, to exist in the misery of pennilessness? How many of us would like to live, as she does, on $24 a week? When the Bible expresses concern for widows and orphans, do you suppose this means that we are meant to act responsibly toward all those in similar circumstances of need and relative helplessness? Should such responsibility toward the needy be exercised through government, the church, or our own personal charity? Or through all three? Is there a danger, when we expect government or a charitable organization to take care of those in need, of our losing the personal contact that love demands? How can we best fulfill the great Commandment, "You shall love your neighbor as yourself"?*

OLDER PEOPLE: What Can We Do?

Except during rush hours, persons sixty-five years or older can ride the subways and buses of New York City at half fare. In San Francisco they can travel on buses and cable cars for a fare of five cents. And older San Franciscans may enjoy full-course meals for only one dollar each. Restaurant owners in the western city have found they could make money by offering dollar lunches and dinners to senior citizens, and their employees enjoy helping the often neglected members of the community.

Japan observes an annual "Respect for the Aged" Day. Do we respect the aged in our cities? What could we do through local laws or programs to help? Does your church take any special interest in its over-65 members, or in those of this age in the community? Do you?

OPEN MINDS

The young British poet Roger Jones wrote a poem about handing out pamphlets on a street corner. One man he hands a pamphlet to hands him one of his own and he thinks about this free exchange of ideas: "Great! That's democracy for you." Then he tears up the stranger's pamphlet without reading it.

Isn't this a perfect picture of the closed mind? Is our religion a matter of handing out prepackaged ideas without being willing to consider fairly what the other person says or thinks? Was Jesus like that?

OPENNESS, FREEDOM, AND HEALTH

One of the daring young writers in modern Russia is Alexander Solzhenitsyn, who likes to write about what he knows about: for example, the bestial conditions at the labor camp where he was imprisoned for eight years.

Superpatriots in Russia cannot understand why Solzhenitsyn wants to run the country down. "Even if there are or were conditions in Russia like that," they ask, "why write about them?" So the Russian Writers' Union expelled their fellow-author late in 1969. On November 10 of that year, Solzhenitsyn wrote the Union a letter explaining his philosophy of truth.

He said the watches of Russia were running centuries slow, its curtains shutting out the dawn that is rising on the outside world. He remined his writer-comrades of the shameful time when Pasternak was shouted down, and said that the blind still lead the blind.

Solzhenitsyn urged his comrades to remember that their first loyalty was to humanity. Humans, he said, differ from animals through thought and speech; when these are restricted, we return to the animal level.

He called for honesty and openness and publicity as indispensable conditions for a healthy society. He warned that without these, a nation cannot be cleansed of its ills but will drive them inside to rot.

Is Solzhenitsyn right? If the great difference between humans and animals is thought and speech, isn't it a step backward to prohibit these—to stop people from thinking their own thoughts and putting them into words? Yet many people applauded, while many others expressed the gravest concern, when American officials recently blasted the newspapers and television networks for criticizing (very charitably and moderately, it seemed to us) what they said.

What is the alternative? Government control of the news media, expressing only what the government wants expressed? Newsmen who do nothing but wave banners for applause after a government official's speech, never daring to differ with anything in it? We had thought that America had something to do with freedom of speech and thought. Must we come finally to totalitarianism?

There is a fresh breeze, a wind of freedom, blowing in Russia today, and in America. When someone like Solzhenitsyn voices it in Russia, he is called names like "bourgeois capitalist" (even if he is not). When someone draws attention to the sores and scabs he sees on America, must he be called a Communist or a Socialist or a radical? Would it be helpful if we stopped calling names and gave attention to the thing complained about?

It has taken the twentieth century to show us that hiding things away doesn't help anyone. When a person represses his natural instincts, he courts madness. (He may need to suppress them, to control them, but it is psychically dangerous to push them out of consciousness.) Unless a disease is treated, it may kill the patient.

Yet when a man tells the society he lives in, "Look! There's something rotten there! Let's do something about it!" he is likely to find everyone acting as though the one who is telling it created the mess.

Unless we are willing to look at our faults, how can they be remedied? There are churches where things are rotten and have been for years. Who is to excise the cancer? There are things in American life that need to be brought into public consciousness—the shameful way we often treat our native Americans, the Indians, on their dwindling reservations; the atrocities we permit to be committed against the people in our prisons;

the way we load the cards of justice against those who are poor or dark-skinned.

Honesty, openness, freedom, health of spirit—do we want these things, or would we rather hide the malignancies that corrode and doom?

PAST: The Good Old Days?

"Why can't things be the way they used to be?" asks an advertisement from *Religion in American Life,* picturing an early-vintage open-top automobile, the kind one sees now in auto museums and antique-car parades.

Why does change have to be? Well, people asked the same question when the first autos appeared; and before that, when locomotives and steamboats were invented; and before that, when printing presses came into being. Change is part of life. We can't go back, but we can go into the future with the God who loves us always.

The real history of "the good old days" suggests that the past was as full of problems and despair as the present. It's tempting to look back at an idealized past which had little to do with the often drab and disappointing realities. It's more a challenge to faith to ask what we can do to make the present more livable, the future more hopeful.

Why does religion so often cling to the past? Should it? What is a Christian's responsibility toward the age we are in and the future?

PATRIOTISM AND FAITH: Opportunity vs. Obedience

Dietrich Bonhoeffer was a loyal German, but his first loyalty was to God and the church of Christ. When Hitler began interfering with the churches and humiliating the Jews, Bonhoeffer felt that he had no choice but to resist and protest. He

154

refused to take part in the state churches which bowed to the Nazi government's demands.

Some of the pastors and theological students argued that they would lose the opportunity of preaching the gospel to the people in the state churches if they followed Bonhoeffer's example. To which the man who was loyal first to God replied, "One act of obedience is better than a hundred sermons."

Witnessing with words is admirable. But it is false witness if every action of our lives does not shout, "I believe in God! All men are brothers in Christ, and I am his undeserving but utterly devoted servant!"

Who said, "To obey is better than sacrifice . . ."? Does I Samuel 15:1–23 throw light on this statement? Might an American face a conflict of faith and patriotism? Is anything more important than the will of God?

See also AMERICA, CHRISTIANITY.

PATRIOTISM, INSTANT

In his novel *The Dakota Project* Jack Beeching has as a central character a technical writer, Dick Conroy, who is instructed: "Prepare a leaflet suitable, after translation into the vernacular, for distribution to (a) Buddhists (b) Muslims, inviting them to volunteer for a nonmilitary venture, details undisclosed, from which they might never return, but which would advantage, not only the economy of their native country, but also the well-being of their co-religionists everywhere."

Dick's Muslim leaflet appeals as follows: "All true believers are brothers. For his brother, as for his faith, a true believer will lay down his life. . . . Those few destined by the will of Allah to return from our enterprise will speak of the great good it has done [here insert Egypt, Syria, Tunisia, Morocco, Iraq, Yemen, etc. etc.] and for Islam. The many who never return will have made a splendid death."

Cynically, Dick prepares the same leaflet for each Muslim

country; only the name of the country need be inserted to provide instant patriotism as an appeal. There are true patriots who deeply love their countries, and there are cynics who use patriotism for their own advantage. Instant patriotism is instantly disposable, like a toilet tissue. Real patriotism is hard-won, not easily dropped, its roots deep in things like faith and conscience.

What is patriotism? Does a true patriot ever criticize his country? Should he always obey every law? Would Jesus have said, "America first"?

For further information: Books by Dietrich Bonhoeffer; *Christianity and Power Politics* by Reinhold Niebuhr; Romans 13:1–7; Acts 5:17–26; Jeremiah 26:1–15.

PEACE: Don't Pray for It!

We were a bit shocked at first sight of this title on an editorial in our favorite "foreign" publication, Canada's *United Church Observer:* "Don't pray for peace." Listen, though, to what the editor said:[1]

"There is too much sentimental talk and too many futile prayers for peace on earth.

"There won't be peace in the world while injustice reigns and the means to correct injustice are ignored, flouted and obstructed by those who profit by injustice and rationalize their profiteering by claims of being better than men of other races, religions or colors.

"We have not the right to pray for or expect peace in Rhodesia, South Africa, Angola or Israel-occupied Jordan, or expect the peoples of those lands to submit to the conqueror and exploiter. We cannot expect the dispossessed of Georgia, Harlem, Halifax, Toronto or Vancouver to remain docile in their slums.

"It is justice to his fellows that God requires of man. Jesus

[1] *United Church Observer,* September 15, 1969, p. 10. Used by permission.

told a man who remembered that a brother had something against him, when he brought his gift to the temple, to leave it and first be reconciled with his brother before offering it at the altar. That applies to us now.

"When we offer our food for the world's hungry, our old clothes for the world's poor, our prayers for the world's peace, we should listen to what the Word says now. We'll hear the Master speaking through the voices of the poor, 'We want justice.'

"There is no prayerful road to peace. There is a rocky road to justice. After we have climbed that road to some sort of rough-hewn justice for all peoples, we will have the right to pray for and expect peace."

Which reminds us of something the British preacher and Bible expositor G. Campbell Morgan had to say about peace when he was pastor of Westminster Chapel in London. Asking why the world was in turmoil, he gave this answer: false patriotism. ". . . the patriotism that consents, out of a narrow attitude of mind, to use the word foreigner. Is there a more terrible word in existence than the word foreigner? . . . The patriotism that says, so long as this land and this country is maintained in peace and prosperity, then it matters nothing what others go down in the struggle, is false, it is of hell! . . . What has Christ to say? . . . He is against everything that denies the absolute right of all men and all nations, and castes, and rulers, to God, and to the fellowship of their brother man. And there will be long conflict ere peace can be established. A peace based upon unfairness and injustice in thinking and attitude towards other nations is no peace, and cannot live or last."[2]

Should we pray for peace until we have done our utmost toward the kind of justice these men are speaking about? Should we expect to avoid atomic obliteration as long as two thirds of the world are perpetually hungry, and the colored peoples feel helplessly humiliated by the whites? Compare what Isaiah had to say in 32:17, and Jesus in Matthew 5:9.

[2] *Westminster Pulpit*, Vol. V, Revell Company.

PEACE: The Peace Symbol vs. the Real Battle

Early in 1970, several publications attacked the well-known peace symbol, denouncing it as, among other things, the sign of the devil, the broken cross, the witch's foot, the Communist peace sign, and the mark of antichrist. To the best of our knowledge, the modern peace symbol originated in England in 1958. It was designed for the Aldermaston Peace Walk from the two signals in the semaphore code for the letters N and D, signifying Nuclear Disarmament; the circle is said to represent the world. To most of the people who use the peace symbol it means nothing more nor less than the desire for peace on earth.

Once when St. Paul was on trial he cried out, "I am a Pharisee!" and brought the men who had accused him—Pharisees and their bitter enemies, Sadducees—into bitter controversy between themselves. They forgot the purpose of the trial as they fought each other. It would be a shame in the 1970s if the symbol of peace became a bone of contention when our efforts should be united against those who have an interest in making war. Our real battle is with the allied forces of labor, business, and the military which President Eisenhower warned us against: "the military-industrial complex." We ought not to be distracted by disputes over symbols.

What does the Bible say about peace? Who is the Prince of Peace? What can we do about peace?

For reference: Isaiah 9:6; Micah 4:1–4; John 14:27, II Corinthians 13:11.

PEACE ON EARTH: A Christmas Prayer

Although spending more for defense than any other country in history, the United States has not been able to keep out of war. As the 1970s began, Americans had been drawn into foreign wars four times in fifty years, and we were still spending more than seventy billion dollars a year on strictly military items. It became increasingly clear that "Except the Lord build the house, they labour in vain that build it: except the Lord keep the city, the watchman waketh but in vain" (Psalm 127:1).

Helen Steiner Rice, the Cincinnati poet whose verses have touched hearts around the world, has written a Christmas prayer that expresses some important truths about peace.

A CHRISTMAS PRAYER FOR PEACE[1]

Our Father, up in heaven,
    hear this Christmas prayer:
May the people of *All Nations*
    be United in Thy Care,
For earth's peace and man's salvation
    can come only by Thy Grace
And not through bombs and missiles
    and our quest for outer space . . .
For until all men recognize
    that "The Battle Is the Lord's"
And peace on earth cannot be won
    with strategy and swords,
We will go on vainly fighting,
    as we have in ages past,
Finding only empty victories
    and a peace that cannot last . . .
But we've grown so rich and mighty
    and so arrogantly strong,
We no longer ask in humbleness—
    "God, show us where we're wrong" . . .
We have come to trust completely
    in the power of man-made things,
Unmindful of God's mighty power
    and that *He is "King of Kings"* . . .
We have turned our eyes away from *Him*
    to go our selfish way,

[1] From *Christmas Classics: Old and New Favorites*. Used by permission of the author.

And money, power and pleasure
　　are the gods we serve today . . .
And the good green earth God gave us
　　to peacefully enjoy,
Through greed and fear and hatred
　　we are seeking to destroy . . .
Oh, Father, up in heaven,
　　stir and wake our sleeping souls,
Renew our faith and lift us up
　　and give us higher goals,
And grant us heavenly guidance
　　as Christmas comes again—
For, more than *Guided Missiles*,
　　all the world needs *Guided Men*.

*Is it true that peace won only with "strategy and swords"
cannot last? Why? Are we destroying "the good green earth"?
Where are we to find "guided men"? Is it possible that they
are right in our midst, that God is waiting to show us what
to do? How can we be guided correctly? Can ordinary people
do anything for peace?*

See also INFLATION, WAR.

PERSISTENCE AND SUCCESS: The WDS Club

Martin Saidel, of Emerson, New Jersey, does not enjoy
inhaling the tobacco smoke from other people's lungs. In a
former generation he might have been called a crank or a
fanatic. In 1969, when he was elected to his town's borough
council, he proposed that smoking be prohibited during council
meetings. All the townspeople at the meeting laughed, thinking
Saidel was joking.

He wasn't. He had going for him the fact that more and
more evidence links smoking with cancer and other diseases,
even when it enters the lungs secondhand. Enough of the

truth had gotten around that the nonsmokers realized his proposal might be a good thing. Who wants to lose a lung because the fellow next to him loves to suck on Cancer Kings? Saidel worked for a year. He organized a WDS Club for people who stood on the platform, "We Don't Smoke." He hung posters around the council room to remind those present how easy it is to die for a smoke.

The opposition did not give in easily. One councilman said the campaign was an invasion of his rights—apparently oblivious of other people's rights to live. When the resolution came to a vote early in 1970, the mayor, who served as council chairman, was smoking a cigarette. The council split three to three, and it was up to the mayor to cast the deciding vote. The result was a compromise of sorts: smoking only during smoke breaks, while the council adjourns.

It took Councilman Saidel a year to get his proposal adopted. Success seldom comes that fast. But the fellow who knows what he wants and keeps at it usually gets there in time.

Why do so many good causes fail? Why did Jesus say that "the people of this world are much more shrewd in handling their affairs than the people who belong to the light" (Luke 16:8, TEV)? Could it be because the people who belong to the light are often careless, lazy, or only half-committed to their cause? What is the main factor for success in anything? What other factors are important?

See also CIGARETTES AND HUMOR, COURTESY AND TOBACCO, SUCCESS.

PHILOSOPHY OF LIFE: Headache Cure

To those who merely read his books, Dr. Nels F. S. Ferré may be only a name in philosophy or theology. To his students and his friends, however, he is known as a most warm and loving personality.

Dr. Ferré once had a pounding headache. He used the occasion to write out his philosophy, and these lines emerged:

> The truth which cannot alter,
> The hope that cannot fail,
> The faith that cannot falter,
> The peace which shall prevail,
> The strength which God has promised,
> The life his love made real,
> I leave unto his keeping
> Come woe or come weal.[1]

Thereupon, Dr. Ferré says, "I exchanged the headache for a joyful heart."

What is your real philosophy—the faith and hope that you cannot doubt? Would meditating on it help your headache? What gives greater joy than a radiant uplook?

For reference: Psalm 51; II Corinthians 12:7–10.

PLEASURE: How Important?

Without any doubt, pleasure is important. Contented cows give more milk, and societies function best when the citizens are given a chance to pursue happiness. There are even philosophies of life built on pleasure; it has been argued that no one really does anything except for his own happiness, and that seeming exceptions such as martyrs or heroes act the way they do to fulfill a psychic need for sacrifice—getting their pleasure out of pain and death. Such notions about man do far less than justice to his depth, complexity, and capacity for genuine love.

But pleasure is better than misery, everything else being equal. When the City of Philadelphia started a new "school without walls," letting each student choose his own course of study and using the city's churches, industries, and other institutions in

[1] *Making Religion Real* by Nels F. S. Ferré, p. 25. Copyright © 1955 by Harper & Row, Publishers, Inc. Reprinted by permission of the publishers.

place of schoolrooms, there were twenty applications for every opening in the new program. Still, some parents worried that the students were not getting the educational essentials they needed. One of the sponsors admitted: "To just make the students happy and deny them the skills they need to survive in a technological society, well, that's not fair."

The point is well-taken. Most churches are run by majority rule. *What happens if what the majority wants or likes is not what it needs? Religious education for children and young people often follows the principle, "Keep them happy." What if there are skills or attitudes or facts they need for survival in a moral universe? Are they getting what they need, or only something to enjoy? Are these two things necessarily different? Are they necessarily the same?*

Jesus said a lot about happiness. Among his statements see Matthew 5:1–12; Mark 8:34–38; John 14:1–6.

POLITICS AND PRINCIPLES: Prince Juan Carlos

Prince Juan Carlos, personally chosen by dictator Franco to succeed him as head of the Spanish government, may not live up to the Generalissimo's expectations. Some people say that Carlos wants to help Spain become a democracy with true freedom. The heir apparent says, "I am Franco's heir, but I am Spain's heir as well."

Should a man put the good of his country ahead of politics? What if he has a boss who insists that only through politics (as usual) can he really help his country? What principles should guide a person in politics? Can a Christian be a politician? Why, or why not? What does politics need most?

POLLUTION AND US

Meet the average American: "Every year he will leave in his wake his share of the 20 million tons of paper, 48 billion cans and 26 billion bottles that litter the land. He will personally pollute three million gallons of water in a year. He will pour enormous amounts of gases into the air from his car and other machines.

"Measured in terms of destructive effect on the environment, biologist Wayne David estimates that 1 American is equivalent to at least 25 citizens of India. Figuring it this way, 205 million Americans are now putting a drain on the resources of the earth that it would take 5 billion Indians to duplicate. And by the same reckoning, our population growth is far more dangerous to the survival of future generations than the much higher rate of China or Mexico."[1]

"The villains of the pollution problem are consumers who demand (or at least let themselves be cajoled into desiring) new, more, faster, bigger, cheaper playthings without counting the cost in a dirtier, smellier, sicklier world. To paraphrase Walt Kelly's Pogo: 'We have met the enemy, and he is us.' "[2]

We must reverse the destructive pollution of everything around us. How? Can one person's efforts help? What can each of us do in the next twelve months?

See also STEWARDSHIP, POLLUTION AND THE FUTURE.

POOR PEOPLE: National Parks?

"When my wife and I were in South Africa, we visited Kruger National Park, a vast expanse of 8000 square miles which had been reserved for elephants, lions and other wild animals. If such a Garden of Eden can be set aside for the free use of animals, it is not unreasonable to make large tracts of land available for the free use of another of God's creatures— dispossessed man. To open our hands liberally to the children of those who served sixty times six years is not reparation; it is decency and wisdom and love."

[1] Robert O'Neil in a WCBS-TV editorial, February 9, 1970.
[2] *Newsweek*, "The Ravaged Environment," a Special Report, March 9, 1970.

So wrote Clarence Jordan to some friends just two days before he died in October 1969. Dr. Jordan had already begun such a "Garden of Eden" project at Koinonia, the experimental Christian farm in Georgia where he spent much of his life. He made farmland and dwellings available to poor families at a nominal sum of something like $25 a month, and would have liked to have made them rent-free. Actually, the rent went into a fund to buy more land for the same purpose.

Is it more important to preserve wildlife (and we believe this is important) than human life? Is it fair and just for some people to have no place to go, nothing to do, no possessions of their own? What would Jesus do?

POOR PEOPLE AND THE BIBLE

What does the Bible have to say to us about the poor, besides the injunction of Paul: "If any would not work, neither should he eat"? (Perhaps this verse is often misread. If my grandfather left me a million dollars, should I be excluded? Should we take that statement of Paul's literally and put men and women of wealth to work?)

A Baptist minister in Edmonton, Canada, answered our first question so beautifully in the *Western Catholic Reporter* of January 18, 1970, that we reproduce his words here. He is the Reverend E. M. Checkland, minister of Edmonton's First Baptist Church.[1]

"In response to the apparently solicitous disciples' concern for the poor, Jesus said: 'The poor you have always with you, but me you do not have always with you.' Here, he was making a fundamental comment upon human nature and upon human society.

"Concerning human society he was saying that poverty is a function of civilization. Never in the history of mankind has any civilization been able to eliminate poverty. Indeed, poverty

[1] "What the Bible Says About the Poor." Used by permission of the publishers.

165

has been the stone upon which every civilization has been built. The poor are always with us because civilization requires that they be. No other conclusion can be drawn from human history as it has been lived on this planet.

"Civilization has been built upon the backs of the poor. The classic examples of this are the slave and the serf upon whose tortured muscles and tormented minds the glories of the past were built.

"But we do not lack for modern instances of the same inhumanity. The wealth, power and comfort of the North Atlantic world are established upon the depressed conditions of people in Asia, Africa and Latin America. We like to think that it is due entirely to our own virtues, energy and know-how. But this is false. It rests more upon the misery of others than it does upon our own virtues. This is the meaning of Nigeria-Biafra and Vietnam. 'To save the village it was necessary to destroy it.'

"Our Lord in making his comment concerning the poor was but stating succinctly one of the fundamental themes of the Bible. He was, in fact, speaking the truth about men and about God. Men, not God, make other men poor, but it is God who sustains the poor so that they do not perish from the land. The mercy of God defeats the malevolence of men, and the continuing presence of the poor is the sign and symbol of the person of God in human history to judge the oppressor and to redeem the oppressed.

"Such is the meaning of his rescue of slaves and his choice of them as his particular and peculiar people. Such also is the meaning of their banishment to exile by God when they refused to accept and obey the implications of their being chosen from slavery as a people for his name.

"Nothing is more stupid than to try to explain poverty away as the inevitable consequence of some vast impersonal process. Like the equally stupid alternative that holds that poverty is the result of the failures of the poor, this is a mere cop-out from responsibility. Persons, not the process, create poverty.

"If you do not think so, I suggest you read the Bible closely and note how throughout all its sixty-six books there is never a word of criticism of the poor. But what criticism of the rich and what attacks upon them! Apart from the love and mercy of God there is probably no theme in the Bible more constant than the rapacity of the rich. Civilization is made by men and, as the Biblical writers understand, the prevalence and persistence of poverty is the fundamental comment upon the kind of beings civilized men actually are. That is the significance of the irony of Jesus' coment, 'but me you do not have always with you.'

"Civilized men create poverty for other men because we are not moved and directed by the mind and spirit of Christ. We have been concerned not for others, but for ourselves and that is a concern diametrically opposed to the interests of God. Hence, Jesus' rejection of the pseudo concern of the disciples.

"In the world that now exists it is imperative that the Church regain, by a more responsible use of her goods, the moral base of her witness that she may be able to bring to bear upon the structures of our civilization the judgment and the mercy of God. She can do this only as she clearly understands and witnesses to the attitude of the writers of the Bible to the poor as the chosen and blessed of God and to the poverty of others as the denial not only of those who must endure that poverty but of God himself."

Do you agree with Pastor Checkland about the foundation of civilization? Have you ever gone through the Bible, as he suggests, noting what God has to say about the rich and the poor? What do you think about a minimum income? If you do not like this idea, what do you believe we should do about the poor and hungry in our midst—in our cities, in the country, on Indian reservations—and in the two thirds of the world where very few ever get enough to eat?

POOR PEOPLE AND HEALTH

"In Tulare County, California, poor whites and Mexican-Americans, too proud to go on relief, told of staggering in the fields as planes illegally sprayed pesticides on them. Some two hundred workers are felled or sickened each year despite laws against spraying DDT and other poison where people are working.

"'I took the number of the plane and told the foreman. Nothing happened,' said one worker. Another added wearily: 'What's the use. They don't stop spraying.'"

So reported Jack Anderson in his syndicated newspaper column "The Washington Merry-Go-Round" for January 28, 1970. These and other data, he wrote, may be found in a report of the American Public Health Association (not yet made public) which accuses both federal and community authorities of "health brutality" against nonwealthy Americans. Among the facts in the report are these:

1. Fifteen Indian families have to live on a junk-covered hill with one water faucet among them, in Great Falls, Montana.

2. A black woman watched her baby die as she waited for three hours in the "emergency" room of a Chicago hospital.

3. Another black woman was refused abdominal surgery because she could not repay eleven pints of blood owed to a Cook County hospital.

4. Real estate developers and state and federal governments conspire to permit the once majestic Potomac River to be filled with untreated human excrement, raw sewage, poisonous salmonella bacteria and dead fish, spreading disease far and wide.

5. In Houston, Texas, while astronauts take off for the moon, other humans and their babies live in fear of rats and snakes, and children have already died of diarrhea caused by malnutrition.

"Health care for the poor has broken down," said the two physicians who prepared the report, Dr. Paul Cornely (president of the American Public Health Association) and Dr. Lester Breslow (past president). "We are shocked and still reeling."

We do not like to think of the poor among us—or of the rats in ghetto slums, the hungry babies, the fathers who cannot get jobs, the mothers who cannot get enough welfare money to buy needed food, the working men and women at the mercy of their bosses (and sometimes of their unions). If these conditions do force themselves on our attention, we like to blame them on the "shiftlessness" or the stupidity of the poor and the needy.

Is this a reason to let children hunger, die, or become brain-damaged from malnutrition? Should a cripple in a slum starve because he cannot do ordinary work? What protection would you or I have if we were migrant workers sprayed with deadly pesticides? Should our government use our taxes to fill our waterways with sewage and death?

Should Christians care? If we care, should we do anything? If we cared enough, would we?

PRAYER: Do We Need Rules?[1]

"Sometimes when I'm scurrying around like a one-woman circus with about six acts going at once, I have this idea cross my mind that I ought to sing more, that I should now and again make joyful noises unto my Lord. And especially when I'm catching my wind and having a word with the Almighty, I get this feeling almost to the point of urgency. But I don't. It seems a silly idea. Who has time to sing anyway? And when I propped a song book up once and tried it, it fell over in the cake batter. Let it wait till we get a piano, I said. And then I got this funny feeling, like maybe I don't quite deserve a piano if I'm going to go at it that way. Or worse still, that the piano will be a painful disappointment. Sort of like waiting till you're married to be happy, only to find that happy is what you take into a marriage, not what you extract from it.

"Anyway, it happened that I sat down at my sewing machine in good faith one day recently to alter a dress for my husband's office party that night. The machine wouldn't sew. I kicked it a little and blew on the offending mechanism and considered the possible operative value of a good cry. Finally I said to God,

[1] The following excerpt is by Emily A. Swinnerton and is used by permission of the author.

Lord, if you'll get this bloody thing to work, why, when I'm done I'll sing you a song!

"Well, it worked . . . Don't ask me to explain that part. Those things happen now and again and all I can say is I don't understand God any more than I understand sewing machines or sunsets . . . And when I was done, well, there was the baby to put down for a nap, and then something got spilled, and really, it was so easy to forget, just like all the other times I'd intended to sing and got sidetracked.

"Then suddenly I stopped in the middle of the whole chronic mess that is housewifery, got the hymnal and sat down at the kitchen table and sang. Now, I haven't anything to offer as a singer, but I'm game to try, so I sang and sang and sang. Once I got going I didn't want to quit!

"I sang from an old Methodist hymnal, and while I am not at the moment a Methodist, I'd like to say that those Methodists have some of the jolliest, rollickingest hymns you ever sang!

"Well, now, if you are wondering what is the point of this whole recital, the point is not that God works in mysterious ways his wonders to perform, or that singing is a heady activity good for the health of the soul. No, the thing all this is about is that I bargained with God. And that's supposed to be a no-no. And when our eldest asked if anything interesting happened to me today and I told her, I felt compelled to add, 'Of course, they say you are not supposed to bargain with God,' just so's to keep her in touch with the ways of the world. Her reply was quite unencumbered by man's rules for man. She said in some exasperation, 'Oh, for heaven's sake, Mother, just be yourself!'

"So I'm here to tell you that if you get hooked on this prayer thing and in your hunger you begin to read everything you can find, why in no time at all you can collect enough rules and do's and don'ts to fill a book. Just like that. And I always say, it's tough to pray when you feel like a pretzel.

"I remember once when I said, God, I know I shouldn't feel this, or say that, or do whatever when I pray, but the fact is, I've just got to talk to you! His reply was quite gracious. He said, 'My lady, will you kindly put away all those great big books and forget them. And when you're anchored enough to read them without losing your balance, and when I'm ready to have you read them, well, then I'll let you know.'

"So my point is that there are all these rules. And if you let them scare you, if you let *them* tell you what to do and not God, and if you revere them and are in awe of them, then, ducks, you are taking your orders from the wrong quarters and revering and awe-ing the wrong thing. And if you say there is truth in all those rules, you are right. But his truth is bigger than all those little truths shooken together and running over.

"So if someone says, Don't bargain with God, well, bargain with God and see what happens. If you read that you shouldn't come to God with an unforgiving heart, why, run right up to him the minute your heart's unforgiving. Where else were you planning to take it? And of course we all know how wicked it is to threaten God. But then, it's not nice to pick on someone smaller than you are either, and a fellow can waste a lot of time looking for an adversary that's just the right size.

"So if you've got a heart-felt threat or two, let fly. He can take it. It will not only help to *not* start a war, or threaten your marriage, or put a last straw on any camel's back. It will give him a chance to exchange it for coin you can use, for something you can build with and mend with and spend in the name of love.

"If it's God you want, don't let anything get in your way, particularly an obstacle labeled 'Helper.' If it's too high to leap over, then just waltz around it. If that doesn't work, then turn and walk the other way. Don't forget, God is behind you as well as before you, and underneath to show you the way."

What would happen if there were a one-year moratorium on books, sermons, and advice about prayer, and instead of discussing it we simply did it?

Sometimes "the exception proves the rule." Are there any rules about prayer to which there may be no exceptions?

If God wanted us to live by rules and regulations, wouldn't

*he have put more of them into the Bible? What does he say
about the rules and regulations that are there?*

Consider these passages: Matthew 22:34–40; Romans 8:1–
17; 13:7–10; Galatians 3:–16:2.

See also HONESTY.

PRAYER: How?

Are there any rules for prayer? Perhaps none in the sense of a
formula, but religious journalist Louis Cassels has gathered seven
suggestions for prayer from Christians through the ages. In the
December, 1969, issue of *The Episcopalian* he suggests:

1. "Pray each day at the same time"—whether it's morning,
evening, or midday.

2. "Have a regular place" to pray. To be able to be alone
can assure necessary concentration.

3. Posture "may make a great difference." Whether it's kneel-
ing, standing, or something else, a posture that is not too relaxing
may help prepare one psychologically to pray.

4. "Prepare for prayer with a brief period of devotional
reading."

5. "Pray as long as you need to or want to—and no longer."
The time should be long enough for your needs, but Scripture
commends brevity.

6. "Pray whether you 'feel like it' or not." Emotions count
less than will and intention with God.

7. "Do not be ashamed to offer 'selfish' prayers, or to seek
God's help in 'little' things." Jesus encouraged his disciples to
pray for bread as well as for the doing of God's will on earth.

*Does the Bible give any rules about praying? Does it offer
principles that are still applicable today? Are there any examples
of prayer we should not follow? What is the purpose of prayer?*

For reference: Matthew 6:5–15; 18:20; 26:39; 26:41;
Mark 9:29; 12:40; Luke 9:29; 11:5–13; 18:1–14; Philippians
4:6; Ephesians 6:10–20; I Thessalonians 5:17.

PRAYER: Is It Answered Wholesale?

The mail brings a printed letter from a famous religionist. The label looks addressographed. Did the religionist buy my name from what is called a "sucker list"? The man says in the letter that he has been praying and that God told him a great healing is coming: "He said it is going to touch your life. . . ."

A stamped, self-addressed envelope is enclosed for my contribution. But I am curious. *How did God tell this man about me? Did he say he was going to touch everyone in the sucker list, or in all the lists? That doesn't sound very personal. I don't doubt that God can work wholesale if he chooses, but I am skeptical about some of his name-droppers. My Bible is full of divine-human encounters, but they are usually between God and one person at a time. Is prayer a matter of visions and revelations, or is it primarily something else?*

PRAYER: What Is It?

One thing that meant much to our forefathers is often quite a puzzle to many of us in the twentieth century. I am talking about prayer. It would seem that prayer meetings in churches and family devotions at home are a thing of the past.

For the 1970 Week of Prayer for Christian Unity, Dr. Roy Neehall wrote an article suggesting that prayer is three important things:[1]

"1) *To pray is to see.* Though the eyes are closed, the mind, heart and soul of the sincere man at prayer are opened to the realities of human need.

"Behold the tragic scene! Millions grow poorer each day while a few amass great wealth. Disease stalks the undernourished while the dustbins of the wealthy overflow. Death comes early to ease the pangs of hunger while the affluent build homes

[1] "The World Calls Man to Prayer," Ecumenical Press Service, October 23, 1969.

in which to put their lonely, unwanted, aged. Whole nations are kept in serfdom by a few unscrupulous families. Powerful minorities buy arms to keep powerless majorities in subjection. Men walk the land aimlessly with no hope of employment. Women wash their crying babies with the tears of despair. Children with inquiring minds never see a schoolroom or a book. People of color are treated like animals, and laws are passed to domesticate them and keep them in ghettos. Businessmen sit in board rooms and manipulate the prices of cocoa, coffee, cane sugar and citrus so those who planted and harvested them will always live on pennies. Governments spend billions on moon landings and sophisticated weapons but can afford only a pittance to aid sagging Third World economies. Large corporations extract the birthright of poor people for a mess of pottage. These are the grim realities we see when we close our eyes in prayer. These are the conditions of the world in which God works. And to work for him is to go where the action is.

"2) *To pray is to act.* The sincere man at prayer may kneel, but not for long. He rises up to join his Lord in the work for development, justice and peace.

"The specter of man's misery and the catalogue of the nations' woes would cause nothing but regret if the world did not possess the means to create change. But we now have the resources. Our wealth includes the science, technology and education to insure every man the dignity of a human being. . . .

"But the church's task goes beyond the material. Men need more than bread if they are to grow, develop, change and become responsible world citizens. The spiritual dimension, which is the ground of hope; the moral factor, which is the expression of love; and the human personality, which is the form of Christ's presence, must command equal attention.

"Men must kneel before they rise. Then action will be of God. Work will be for God. Men of God will be at work with God, where the action is.

"3) *To pray is to unite.* The hands of the man at prayer are clasped. Unclasped, they must join the hands of other men and women of good will to overcome evil with good.

"The realities we confront are enormous. Isolated skirmishes are ineffectual. . . . If we would root out the causes rather than merely dab at the symptoms of man's misery, then we must act together. . . .

"There is much to do, much to overcome and much to change. God has used man before to challenge the principalities and powers, the structures of injustice and the systems of inhumanity. But the modern world is a complex of conflicting loyalties, and a disunited, disjointed, disparate effort is doomed to failure.

"In prayer we see the issues, by prayer we are moved to act, and in the same unity of spirit which drives us to pray together we unite to follow and to work with Christ where the action is."

Do you agree? Does prayer help us to see things more clearly? Does it help us act more effectively? Is religion exclusively a personal relationship with God, or is it also a matter of getting into the right relationships with others? Does prayer help people work together better and more successfully? What is prayer in your experience?

PRAYER: What Should We Pray About?

For some of us, it is easy to let the devotional or spiritual life move in a rut. We may pray or meditate in only one area, neglecting all the riches and opportunities elsewhere in the Kingdom of God's grace and power.

In her fascinating little book *Psalms '70,* Mary Perkins Ryan tells us how much the Psalms of David came to mean to her as she moved out into new ways of Christian living. Her book groups these ancient but modern prayers and songs into seven great themes. They follow, slightly adapted, with the hope that they will suggest some of the major directions our prayers and ultimate desires may profitably take.

David cried, "Praise the Lord . . . with the harp of ten strings!" (Psalm 33:2). Here are seven that some of us might pluck more often.

1. *Celebrating the goodness of God.* Is there anyone who has not been stirred to thankfulness by a fresh spring day, an autumn landscape, an indescribable sunset, a great act of courage, a heroic life, a moving play or book or concert or painting? How did it come about, if not ultimately from God? "With thanksgiving," Paul wrote to the Philippian Christians, "let your requests be made known to God" (Philippians 4:6).

2. *Hungering for justice.* When we are sickened by learning of hunger, of cruelty in public institutions, of political corruption, of tortures and massacres, of the degrading of human beings, of the destruction of living creatures and our environment, of the obscenities of war, of the weak and poor ground down to fatten the rich and powerful, those whose souls harbor any flicker of the candle of the Lord yearn for justice. Then we may cry out with the Psalmist, "Help, Lord" (Psalm 12:1)!

3. *Longing for vitality.* No one is without low moods; depression, fear, apathy, joylessness, despair strike many. At such times, when we feel furthest from God, we need most to level with the Infinite and wait for the assurance of his presence.

4. *Complaining to God.* Here we face an aspect of life from which traditional religion may recoil. Job's friends were shocked when he dared to express his misgivings and doubts about the way God seemed to be running the universe, but his vitality of integrity was truer than their blindfolded piety. Staggered by the wasting away of his beloved wife, Alan Paton wondered whether God is, after all, as the Hindus think, both Brahma and Siva, both Creator and Destroyer. "I suppose this may be blasphemy," he wrote in *For You Departed,* "but it is at least honest blasphemy." The Psalms encourage us to tell God exactly how we feel about him. "Giving vent to our real feelings in God's presence," writes Mary Ryan, "even when they aren't 'religious' feelings, is better than being unreal with God, which leads us to be unreal with ourselves and with others."

5. *Turning back to God.* The Father never closes his door to any prodigal son or daughter. Like the deeper rapport between two lovers after a quarrel is mended, the good news of salvation

seems to reach its highest moments in renewed fellowship with the Eternal One.

6. *Searching for God.* Solomon's beloved heard the young prince knocking at her door, but when she got to it he was gone and her heart sank: "I sought him but I did not find him, I called him but he did not answer" (Song of Solomon 5:6). For some reason, much of our praying seems to have to be longing, looking, listening, searching. Perhaps we would not appreciate his presence so much if he were a robot to be summoned by pushing a button.

7. *Looking forward to the Kingdom.* If we were simply pilgrims on a road that led finally over a cliff into a black void, we might cherish the chances of lightening the way for our fellow travelers. But our highest moments would have for background that final despair. The heartening note that radiates through our faith is the certainty that the Kingdom will come, the battle be won, the age of love and peace finally arrive. "The Kingdom of God is coming wherever love is at work," writes Mary Ryan, and we take courage that love will conquer all. So we work in faith and pray in hope.

When some great good comes our way, do we remember who gives every perfect gift? Do our prayers include remembrance of those who are working to right wrongs, and compassion for those who thoughtlessly injure their brothers? Are we honest enough to bring God our low moments and doubts and even our complaints? Do we doubt that God is always yearning for our return? Do we tend to give up when God seems far away? Do we work and pray in confident hope?

For reference:

1. Celebrating God's goodness—Psalm 95:1–2; Luke 17:17–18; Ephesians 5:20; Philippians 4:4–7, 20; Ephesians 1:3–23.

2. Hungering for justice—Micah 6:6–8; Proverbs 21:3; Amos 5:15; Matthew 5:6.

3. Longing for vitality—Psalms 38:9; 119:131; 3:32; 107:9; Isaiah 55:1; Matthew 5:4.

4. Complaining to God—Job 3; 8:1–3; 42:7; Psalms 39; 88; Luke 6:21.

5. Turning back to God—Luke 15, Psalms 32; 38; 51; Isaiah 1:1-20.

6. Searching for God—Luke 11:9; Philippians 3:12; Psalms 25; 27; 42; 63.

7. Looking forward—Luke 12:32; Matthew 6:9-10; 13: 24-33; Psalm 145:13; Romans 14:17; Isaiah 2:1-4; Revelation 11:15.

PRAYER AND FREEDOM

William McNamara has a theory about why so many people are leaving the church. "They are being served conventional piety and tyrannized by rules when they should be nourished and freed by development of the contemplative spirit," this founder of the Spiritual Life Institute of America said recently.

Prayer and religion are thought of as demanding, forbidding, restrictive. What if they are—at their best and highest and deepest—truly liberating? Are there church members who know rules and conventions when they should know the joy and liberty of freedom in Christ? Do some people leave the church because they never learned what it is all about?

For reference: Isaiah 55:1; John 8:36; Galatians 5:1; James 1:25.

PRISON AND SOCIETY: "Like a Wild Beast . . ."

He had spent time in prisons from Rikers Island, New York, to Soledad, California. The last time he got out, he carried in his pocket a message from another inmate, a letter to society that expresses the feelings of a number of those behind bars:

"You have placed us here for punishment, you say, but the quest for revenge lights your features. Even so, if prison is for punishment, the method derived to inflict that punishment is calculated to strip us of our initiative, decency, pride and respect.

178

"After many years of degradation, humiliation and living a life of intrigue and perversion, you ask me to step from my 'den of iniquity' into your paradise and you expect me to make this transition overnight. I marvel at your naïveté.

"Fate stirs the finger of fear within me. Like a wild beast I shall soon be unleashed to prey amongst you. I have survived my ordeal in this concrete and steel jungle and I am ready for the hunt."[1]

Is it true that the average prison is a place of perversion and degradation? Do you know? Have you read books like Menninger's The Crime of Punishment, *or talked with those behind bars? Do you know what prison life is like in your own state and city? What is the real purpose of imprisonment? How does actual imprisonment carry out that purpose? How did the system of imprisonment begin?*

See also CRIME AND THE POOR, CRIME AND PUNISHMENT.

PROBLEM SOLVING: They and Us

A group of businessmen were discussing some problems for which there seemed no solution. Suddenly one of the men said, "Say, we've all been talking about what 'they' ought to do. How about thinking about what *we* can do?"

They did, and the result was the beginning of a program that made a considerable dent in a problem that had seemed hopeless as long as everyone focused on other people.

At least two things are wrong with the "they" attitude. One is that we are not responsible for what "they" do, but we *are* responsible for what "we" do about a problem. The other is that it is too negative to concentrate on other people's mistakes. Results begin to come when we move into a positive, faith-filled approach: What can *we* do?

Which is easier: gossiping about other people's failures, or

[1] The New York *Times*, February 11, 1970.

planning constructive actions of our own? Basically, are "they" greatly different from "us"? What is the danger in concentrating too much on the mistakes of others?

PROTESTS: Civil Disobedience, Justice, and Change

"We acknowledge that an act of civil disobedience can breed disrespect for law and provoke an outbreak of violence, but we also know that it can be a powerful instrument for the achievement of justice. Without it, Americans would not have many of the root freedoms they now enjoy."—Report of the American Friends Service Committee, November 22, 1968.

"Americans have been practicing [dissent] with vigor since the day George Washington watched veterans of the Revolutionary War demonstrating outside his presidential mansion in Philadelphia. . . . [Fighting protesters with force] can be self-defeating if a nation cannot change peacefully when its people call for change."—Lyndon B. Johnson in 1969 *Encyclopaedia Britannica Book of the Year.*

When is it right to protest, and when is it wrong?

PROTESTS AND DEMONSTRATIONS: In Moscow Too?

America isn't the only place where young people and old make protests and stage demonstrations. From all reports, this sort of thing is happening in every part of the world from Paris to Tokyo to Moscow. A student in Leningrad distributed pamphlets calling for more freedom. Two students in a Moscow department store handcuffed themselves to a railing and scattered leaflets requesting the freeing of Russians imprisoned for opposing the government. Another student distributed leaflets in a Moscow theater. The young people, naturally, were tried and sentenced.

It would be easy to accept the view that student protests in most of the world are Communist-inspired if it weren't for the student protests in Russia, too. The Russians claim it's CIA-inspired, a plot of capitalism. *Could it be that in all these countries it's simply the desire of human beings for peace, freedom, and the things they consider important?*

See also CONFORMITY OR INDIVIDUALISM?

QUITTING

In his fine book *Eight Days That Rocked the World*, Wallace Chappell tells of the evening he was preaching in another church when the pastor called for testimonies from those present. One lady stood up and said that she had once belonged to that church, but there had been so much friction that the Lord led her out. Dr. Chappell, aghast at the cold blanket this threw over the atmosphere, walked to the pulpit and said: "Let us pray. Father God, help us to know you never lead us out of a battle but always into one. Amen."

Does quitting ever help a situation? If there is friction in a church, what should we do? What is one thing Jesus said about hard feelings between brethren? (See Matthew 5:23–24). Is there ever a time to get out of a Christian group? When there are differences of opinion in an organization, when is the time to stick to your guns, and when is the time to give in?

RACE RELATIONS: What Can We Do?

"If we are to continue to make progress in race relations, we must have reasonable citizens, both black and white. We who are white must face the facts and admit that the Negro has been oppressed in many areas. We must confess that during the past century Negroes have been discriminated against in many ways. We must recognize that we live in a new era; that yesterday is past, and all people, regardless of race, creed or color, are entitled to equal rights. . . .

"We must continue to improve our neighborhoods through code enforcement. We must continue the fight to eliminate poverty by giving peoples of all races an opportunity to advance. We must be concerned about the health and welfare of our neighbors. We must keep on providing playgrounds and recreational programs for our young people. We must create such an atmosphere of progressiveness and togetherness that when the Rap Browns and Stokely Carmichaels come along, our people will tell them, 'Don't stop here, for we have a good thing going—a city of all the people, where the war on poverty is working because everyone has an opportunity to work.' "[1]

Mr. Mims is city commissioner of Mobile, Alabama. How does what he says apply to your community? What can you and your neighbors do about race relations? What did the first-century Christians do about a racial problem? (See Acts 6:1–7.)

See also BLACK AND WHITE, BLACKS AND HOPE, AMERICAN INDIANS.

REALIZATION

This title of an article in a religious magazine caught the eye of commuters in a suburban railway station:

TALK LESS AND REALIZE MORE

Talking is an important art. Our age seems to major in words. We destroy more trees to print more newspapers, books, and magazines than anyone anytime in history. Television, radio, government, business, and religion drown us in words. But sometimes we talk ourselves into bed, ulcers, or war. Wise men through the ages have taken time off to be silent and reflect on the meaning and purpose of life.

Are we too busy talking or writing or reading to realize what life is all about, why we are here, what we are doing, how great God is, how wonderful people are, what we can be and do for the highest and best?

[1] Lambert C. Mims, *For Christ and Country* (Fleming H. Revell), pp. 67, 70–71. Used by permission.

"There was a man who had two sons. He went to the older one and said, 'Son, go work in the vineyard today.' 'I don't want to,' he answered, but later he changed his mind and went to the vineyard. Then the father went to the other son and said the same thing. 'Yes, sir,' he answered, but he did not go. Which one of the two did what his father wanted?"

Those are the words of Jesus in *Good News for Modern Man,* the American Bible Society's new translation (Matthew 21:28–31). *What is the answer to his question? Do we realize we are sons and daughters of God, with his infinite possibilities as vast as space in every direction?*

For reference: I Corinthians 6:19–20; Ephesians 1:15–23; 3:14–21; Philippians 4:4–9, 13, 19.

RECONCILIATION AND THE CHURCH

What is the main task of the church? In these days when so many churches are involved in civic affairs, many people are rethinking this question. "Of course," says C. Edward Crowther in his book *Where Religion Gets Lost in the Church,* "it is right for the church to ally herself with civil-rights groups. If the cause is just, then the church must help fight for it. The Christian, however, must be alive to the fact that the ticket bought by many 'secular' civil-rights groups does not take us to the end of the line. If tomorrow the miracle were to occur, and man were able to live at peace with himself and with his brother, the work of the civil-rights groups would have been accomplished. Not so, however, the work of the church. Her main task would remain to be completed, which is man's reconciliation with God."

Do you agree? Which is more important, civil rights or spiritual reconciliation? But how does reconciliation happen? Do you recall Jesus' statement about the relationship of the two kinds of reconciliation, with God and with our brothers? Look up Matthew 5:23–24.

RELIGION: Why Does It Turn People Off?

"For sixteen hundred years the words 'God' and 'Christ' have been used as often to frighten, punish, hurt, deceive, torture, exploit, and kill as to comfort, restore and heal. The long record embracing the tortures of the Inquisition, the crimes of Renaissance popes, the blood baths of the Protestant Reformation, the Salem witch burnings and the Reconstruction racists has left its mark on the public consciousness. For a thousand years the organized churches have been found more consistently on the side of the puppet tyrant, the gouging landowner, the usurious moneylender, the robber baron, the sweatshop prince, the mass briber and the big-scale cheat than on the side of the common worker and suffering mankind. At this point there is too much history to be lived down to expect the churches to find quick and easy restoration to public trust. 'Tell me anything you want to, chum,' is a refrain often heard by the counselor, 'but don't gimme any of that god stuff.' If we are to find some avenue for a general return to God we must open other channels."

So writes the anonymous "Older Member" in the impressive little book *The Light That Heals*.[1] This is a report on a conference on spiritual therapy attended by representatives of churches, hospitals, Alcoholics Anonymous, Camps Farthest Out, and other groups.

Is what the Older Member says here true? Isn't there at least enough truth in it to make us slightly uncomfortable? If religious talk and its associations often turns people off, what other channels of helpfulness are there?

The Older Member says that one thing he finds useful in trying to witness to other people is not to worry too much about *words*. He simply talks to them in their own language so that the barrier of religion will not put them off—until God and Christ are so real to them that the language doesn't

[1] Older Member Press. Box 25, Guilford, Connecticut 06437. Used by permission.

matter any more. When Jesus began talking with the Samaritan woman at a well, the first thing he said to her was, "Give me to drink." He then proceeded from her frame of reference to his—but only as fast as she was able to follow.

Another channel is *personal experience.* Theology and philosophy may be debated forever, but no one can deny what God has done for you in your own life. Telling that, preferably not in pious language, may be more convincing than a ton of sermons.

What other channels have you found helpful in helping others? How can we serve God in a nonreligious age? Would it be better if some of us talked less and practiced our faith more?

RELIGION, SERVICE, AND GOD

The tidal wave of nuns, priests, and ministers who are leaving the church to work in the secular world gives the impression that the departing religious have deserted religion. Have they?

Marylin Bender interviewed a blue-eyed editor of *Glamour* magazine, Midge Turk, who had spent eighteen years as Sister Agnes Marie in a Los Angeles convent. There she was principal of a city high school, Miss Bender reported in the New York *Times* of February 5, 1970 (p. 42), but found her hands tied when she tried to give her students the education they needed. She felt a three-way tug of war; her responsibility to the students clashed with her responsibility to her religious organization, and of course there was her belief. Midge (as she is now called) said, "I believed in helping people. . . . I'd rather be loyal to what I believed in." So out of loyalty to her deepest beliefs ("in humanity, in Christianity"), she left the church to serve God elsewhere. Now she is working in the field of education as college editor of *Glamour.*

Another former nun interviewed by Miss Bender is Dacia Van Antwerp, who now directs an educational company. Dacia says, "I left because God wanted me to. I feel I can do more for him on the outside. I can help the world more."

We believe these two young ladies are representative of most of those who have left full-time church work. Rather than leaving religion, they have left their ecclesiastical jobs for the most profoundly religious reasons: to serve God and people more completely. For God's sake they work in the world.

It used to be widely assumed that a person served God in the church and worked for the devil (or for something in between if he had a job in the world outside). Today there is an emphasis on "secularizing the church" and serving God in the world. We are finding that religion is a seven-day-a-week proposition, that there may be as much politics and corruption in a religious establishment as in a secular one, and that God cannot be put in a box even if there is a steeple on top.

Is this new emphasis sound or unsound? Will it lead to the disintegration of the churches? Where should the action be for a Christian? Is it possible that God leads some people out of the church, and others into it? If there is a conflict between a religious organization and one's conscience, which must have priority? Why?

RESPONSIBILITY: When Should Christians Speak Out?

Late in 1969, news broke of an incredible event. American veterans of the war in Vietnam testified to entering a village in Song My and shooting down unarmed civilians—old men, women, young boys and girls, and babies—as they begged for mercy. The United States Army charged a number of soldiers with the murder of more than a hundred men, women, and children "without justification or excuse." Some said the number killed was 370; some, more than 500. Army photographer Sgt. Ronald L. Haeberle released photographs he had taken during the massacre showing the victims before and after being gunned down.

Many churchmen who had not previously hesitated to denounce hair styles, hem lengths, pay television, and assorted forms of entertainment, or to express their minds on national elections and various national and international affairs, were mysteriously silent. Methodist Bishop Gerald Kennedy and some church leaders called for a day of mourning. Veteran religion reporter Louis Cassels asked a number of clergymen if they would care to make some kind of statement about the Song My (or My Lai) massacre for release in the magazine *Christian Herald*.[1]

More than half the clergymen couldn't or wouldn't be bothered. Among those who could and did were Dr. Ernest T. Campbell, Presbyterian minister of New York's Riverside Church, who said, "We have been feeding on this image of national righteousness and arguing down the instances that argue against it, but truth has finally caught up with us."

Monsignor Marvin Bordelon, director of the Division of World Justice and Peace of the United States Catholic Conference, asked, "What difference does it make if the people of My Lai were mowed down in cold blood or incinerated with napalm or blasted apart with bombs? . . . What is apparent is the systematic annihilation of the Vietnamese people and their land."

Rabbi Maurice N. Eisendrath, President of the Union of American Hebrew Congregations, inquired: "Is it really true, as the President had said, that My Lai is merely an 'aberration' in an otherwise restrained and civilized performance by our troops? Or, instead, is My Lai merely the most spectacular and blood-curdling expression of a cruel and inhuman war which we ourselves measure in body counts; that My Lai personalizes in miniature the slaughter of innumerable other women and children, the destruction of hospitals and schools by the most brutal and widespread bombings in history; that My Lai symbolizes the consequences of our dehumanizing of people by calling them 'gooks,' and signifies the moral bankruptcy in which no one has any clear sense of purpose or meaning in all this bloodshed?"

[1] March 1970. Used by permission.

Rabbi Eisendrath continued, "One must ask: What does it mean when so many Americans denounce the mass media for revealing the massacre, and impugn the patriotism of the brave soldiers who brought forth the truth? What does it mean when Americans defend murderers on the argument that they only followed orders? . . .

"What does it mean when Americans say: But what about the Communist massacres at Hue or elsewhere, as if our moral standards are to be no higher than those of the Communist and Nazi butchers of our time?

"And another question: What kind of a regime are we fighting for in South Vietnam—a regime whose automatic response to revelations of the mass slaughter of its own people is to say it never happened, it's Communist propaganda, it's really nothing. Such a regime is morally bankrupt. It cannot be rescued by the endless flow of American blood."

These are questions to ponder. If the charges of the United States Army are correct, if the testimony of those who have already confessed to their part in the alleged massacre are to be believed, what can one say? But if ever there was a time for Christians to speak, is not this the time?

RESPONSIBILITY IN BUSINESS

Enid A. Haupt, Editor-in-Chief of *Seventeen* magazine, says: "Our readers are very impressionable, not yet cynical about advertising . . . eager to learn . . . to believe. . . . Since *Seventeen* does have such a great influence on our readers, we are selective about what we will accept. As an example, we have never carried cigarette or liquor advertisements or improbable claims such as 'bust developers.'"

Does a service-oriented product such as a magazine have a responsibility to the public? Does a magazine or newspaper have the right to publish falsehoods or to "shade" the truth, either in its editorial columns or in its advertising? What advantages are there in making fraudulent claims in advertising?

What are the disadvantages? Should a magazine print what its readers want to see, or does it have a responsibility beyond this? What is it?

See also BUSINESS AND ETHICS, TRUTH IN ADVERTISING.

RESPONSIBLE ACTION

Dietrich Bonhoeffer was a young German minister who was as horrified at what Hitler and the Nazis were doing during World War II as was the world outside Germany. He came to the conclusion that it was his Christian duty to help get rid of the head of his government—Adolf Hitler—and in 1945 was executed for plotting to assassinate the Führer. In Bonhoeffer's *Letters and Papers from Prison* is this statement about what it means to be a responsible member of society[1]:

"One may ask whether there have ever before in human history been people with so little ground under their feet— people to whom every available alternative seemed equally intolerable, repugnant and futile. . . . The great masquerade of evil has played havoc with all our ethical concepts. For evil to appear disguised as light, benevolence, historical charity or social justice is quite bewildering to anyone brought up on our traditional ethical concepts, while for the Christian who bases his life on the Bible it merely confirms the fundamental wickedness of evil."

Bonhoeffer goes on to cite the failures of several different groups of well-meaning people. "The *reasonable* people's failure is obvious." They think a little reasoning, he says, will fix everything, but while they try to do justice to everyone, "the conflicting forces wear them down with nothing achieved. Disappointed by the world's unreasonableness, they step aside in resignation or collapse before the stronger party."

[1] Reprinted with permission of The Macmillan Company from *Letters and Papers from Prison* by Dietrich Bonhoeffer. Copyright by The Macmillan Company, 1953. © by SCM Press. Ltd., 1967, pp. 16-19.

Another group: *moral fanatics.* "The fanatic thinks that his single-minded principles qualify him to do battle with the powers of evil; but like a bull he rushes at the red cloak instead of at the person who is holding it; he exhausts himself and is beaten. He gets entangled in nonessentials and falls into the trap set by cleverer people.

"Then there is the man with a *conscience,* who fights singlehanded against heavy odds in situations that call for a decision. But the scale of the conflicts in which he has to choose—with no advice or support except from his own conscience—tears him to pieces. Evil approaches him in so many respectable and seductive disguises that his conscience becomes nervous and vacillating, till at last he contents himself with a salved instead of a clear conscience, so that he lies to his own conscience in order to avoid despair. . . .

"From the perplexingly large number of possible decisions, the way of *duty* seems to be the sure way out. Here, what is commanded is accepted as what is most certain, and the responsibility for it rests on the commanders, not on the person commanded. But no one who confines himself to the limits of duty ever goes so far as to venture, on his sole responsibility, to act in the only way that makes it possible to score a direct hit on evil and defeat it. The man of duty will in the end have to do his duty by the devil too.

"As to the man who asserts his complete *freedom* to stand foursquare to the world, who values the necessary deed more highly than an unspoilt conscience or reputation, who is ready to sacrifice a barren principle for a fruitful compromise, or the barren wisdom of a middle course for a fruitful radicalism—let him beware lest his freedom should bring him down. He will assent to what is bad to ward off something worse, and in doing so he will no longer be able to realize that the worse, which he wants to avoid, might be the better. Here we have the raw material of tragedy.

"Here and there people flee from public altercation into the sanctuary of *private virtuousness.* But anyone who does this must shut his mouth and his eyes to the injustice around him.

Only at the cost of self-deception can he keep himself pure from the contamination arising from responsible action. In spite of all that he does, what he leaves undone will rob him of his peace of mind. He will either go to pieces, because of this disquiet, or become the most hypocritical of Pharisees.

"Who stands fast? Only the man whose final standard is not his reason, his principles, his conscience, his freedom or his virtue, but who is ready to sacrifice all this when he is called to obedient and responsible action in faith and in exclusive allegiance to God—the responsible man, who tries to make *his whole life* an answer to the question and call of God."

Does this statement have any relevance for us? How would the different reactions Bonhoeffer outlines work out in practice today? Is it possible to help the world much by the power of reason alone, or by more personal righteousness or the like? Is it possible to offer one's "whole life" in the fight against injustice and evil? What modern individuals are examples of this kind of commitment?

RESURRECTION

Albert Schweitzer, that strange German lover of pipe organs and Jesus, was admired throughout his life by many people and regarded by others with the deepest suspicion. In 1969 Harper & Row published a book of his early sermons entitled *Reverence for Life*. In these messages, delivered mostly before World War I, one catches the great man's simple faith and love. In them there is no suggestion, as Dr. David A. Redding wrote in the January, 1970, *Christian Herald*, of "an old liberal busily removing the foundations of the faith." Instead, the book acquaints us with a man "who would follow Jesus to the ends of the earth. . . . He preaches mostly about happiness and what a comfort 'Our Saviour' is along the way. . . . Schweitzer insists that the preacher's job is not to defend a doctrine but to go and meet 'him.'"

In one of his sermons Albert Schweitzer says, "A man does

nothing for the Lord's sake without being aware that he has done it for a living Lord."

Is there any better proof of the Resurrection than this power of Jesus, two thousand years after he was killed and buried, to grip a man for lifelong dedication, not in doleful misery but in reckless joy? What does this awareness of "a living Lord," of "meeting Him," of walking in the comfort and happiness of His presence, say about His endless Life?

For reference: I Corinthians 15:1–28, 58; Philippians 3: 8–14.

See also DEATH AND RESURRECTION, ETERNITY, IMMORTALITY, JESUS.

REVOLUTION: Was Jesus a Revolutionary?

The same weekend in 1969 that the first men walked on the moon, five thousand Black Panthers held a conference on revolution in Oakland, California. Several of the speakers, including at least one missionary, according to reporter Kathy Mulherin, "described Christ as a revolutionary."

That's a popular way of describing Christ today; at least one book bears the title *Jesus the Revolutionary*. Certainly some of the things he did—organizing an elite cell of twelve men willing to risk their lives, and demonstrating against the temple's oppressive merchandising practices, for example—remind us of certain revolutionary leaders today. If a revolutionary is a person who is not content with the way things are and is willing to lay his life on the line to make them better, Jesus was one.

I'm reminded, however, of the time not too many years ago when a best-selling book described Jesus as a sort of super-salesman. He was that, too, I guess, if you can think of what he did as selling a product (I have a little difficulty, myself, picturing Jesus as an auto salesman). To some, Jesus is an Oriental guru dispensing timeless wisdom. Or a theologian. Or a general. Or many other things.

Is it possible we see in Jesus Christ what we want to see?

Yet he is so much more than any human mold can hold. If your God is a revolutionary *and no more,* your God is too small by billions of galaxies.

Who was Jesus? Albert Schweitzer said that those who obey Him "shall learn in their own experience Who He is." Do you agree?

RIGHT AND WRONG: Aaron and Reality Therapy

Aaron was an eleven-year-old boy whose behavior was described by Dr. William Glasser, his psychiatrist, as horrible. In his book *Reality Therapy,* Dr. Glasser says Aaron was the most obnoxious child he had ever met; the boy would kick, scream, run away and hide, become withdrawn, disrupt his classes, and make everyone disgusted with him.

Dr. Glasser saw one problem with Aaron that no one else observed: "No one had ever told him he was doing wrong." And no one had ever set limits on what he could and could not do. The psychiatrist decided to try a completely new tack. The boy would have to behave, to act reasonably or be punished. He responded remarkably, "probably because he had been anxious for so long to be treated in this realistic way." He became courteous, well-behaved, and his miserable grades went to straight A's. For the first time in his life Aaron began to play constructively with other children, to enjoy honest relationships with others, and to stop blaming his troubles on his mother or other people.

Dr. Glasser calls this "reality therapy" and says one of an individual's greatest needs is to be made to realize that he is personally responsible for what he does, and that right behavior accomplishes more than wrong behavior.

How does all this square with the Bible's emphasis on the moral law, on personal responsibility for our actions, on honesty and right and wrong? Could parents and teachers apply some "reality therapy" to their young charges?

See also COMMANDMENTS AND COURTROOMS, MORALITY.

SACRIFICE: Doing Good May Be Far from Easy

Automobiles today seem to be considerably safer than they used to be largely because of one person: Ralph Nader. His testimony before Congress and his book *Unsafe at Any Speed* provide documentation that certain models were highly defective and could and did cause many accidents. The Corvair, for example, Nader reported, had rear wheels that often bent over so far the rim actually touched the road, causing the car to turn over.

Early in 1970 the highest court in New York State upheld Ralph Nader's right to sue Corvair's manufacturer, General Motors, for what it did after it learned what was in his book. Nader says the giant corporation tried to interview his friends under false pretenses, tapped his telephone, cast aspersions on his integrity and his religious views, harassed him with obnoxious telephone calls in the dead of night, and even arranged for him to be "accosted by girls for the purpose of entrapping him into illicit relationships."

A subcommittee of the United States Senate had invited both Mr. Nader and General Motors to appear before it in connection with its investigation of traffic safety. James Roche, the corporation's president, admitted to the subcommittee that Mr. Nader had suffered "some harassment" and that what the company had done was "most unworthy of American business."

Crusaders for any worthy cause seldom have an easy time of it. Perhaps they shouldn't expect to. Socrates was put to death by his countrymen on charges of corrupting youth. *How many American leaders have been assassinated? How many Biblical personalities served time in jail?*

Jesus once said, "If anyone wishes to be a follower of mine, he must leave self behind; he must take up his cross and come with me. Whoever cares for his own safety is lost . . ." (Matthew 16:24–25, NEB). *Is that true only in a religious sense, or does it also apply to courageous individuals like Ralph Nader? Does it apply to us?*

SCIENCE AND TRUTH: What We Don't Know About the Moon

Before the first men landed on the moon, a number of scientists thought it might be covered with dust—and that humans might sink out of sight in it. All the dust there was turned out to be more like wet sand.

Then, after the historic mission of Apollo 11, it was concluded that all the moon's "sea" areas must be like the Sea of Tranquility. Half of the rocks the first moonwalkers brought from there were made of breccias, material fused together from the impact of meteors. But when Apollo 12 landed in the Sea of Storms, very few rocks contained breccias.

Today, after billions of dollars and man-hours spent in moon exploration, there are more questions than ever about the moon. What we don't know would fill more volumes by far than what we do know.

Science is a marvelous tool. But scientists are the first to acknowledge that science doesn't begin to have all the answers. Its little truths simply show more clearly the outlines of the great truths beyond it. When Jesus said, "I am the truth" (John 14:6), he was not talking about bits and pieces of truth, but about the whole mysterious reality, ultimate truth, the ground of all being, the final foundations of the universe. He claimed to have the secret of life at its deepest and best. Millions of people have found that he has.

SCRIPTURE: Out of Date?

The Bible "does not seem a likely candidate for the best-read book of this generation," Bishop Gerald H. Kennedy of the Methodist Church said at a meeting of the American Bible Society. While people expect it to "tell it like it is," he said, the Bible appears to be out of step with our age; it "tells it like it ain't and, more important, the way it ought to be and will be."

Furthermore, said Bishop Kennedy, it is when we are pleased

with ourselves and our society that the Bible thunders warnings and judgment. But when we realize our sins and feel hopeless, "the Bible reminds us of the great things which have not been affected by modernity and are unchanged and unscathed." So the Book never tells us what we may want to hear, but always what we need to hear.

What is the Bible's central message? If it perfectly satisfied our age, would it, or could it, speak to other ages? If there is a divine message in it (as we believe there is), can it ever leave human beings completely content and undisturbed?

See also THE BIBLE, TROUBLE AND HOPE.

SCRIPTURE AND PROPAGANDA

Early in 1970, a Catholic and a Protestant made a joint protest against using the Bible to egg on either Jews or Arabs in their Mideast conflict. Dr. J. Martin Bailey, Editor of the United Church of Christ's *United Church Herald,* and Father Charles Angell, Editor of the Catholic publication *The Lamp,* wrote an editorial for both publications deploring the use of the Scriptures as propaganda for either side. They expressed chagrin over the "glaring anti-Jewish statements from otherwise respected Christian leaders" as well as the use of Scripture to justify the existence and military ventures of Israel.

It wasn't many years ago that the same Bible was used for and against infant baptism, for and against slavery, for and against government by bishops or deacons, for and against such theological matters as predestination and limited atonement. Scripture was not written to become propaganda for any cause, no matter how well-intentioned.

Why was it written? How should we use the Bible? Does it either glorify or denigrate any side of anything?

For reference: Psalm 119; Luke 24:27; John 10:35; Romans 15:4; II Timothy 3:16.

SELF-RIGHTEOUSNESS

"The real question is not whether we shall have sex education Saints, Joseph Fielding Smith, was quoted in *The Christian Century* as saying of his denomination: "We are, notwithstanding our weaknesses, the best people in the world. . . . We are morally clean, in every way equal and in many ways superior to any other people."

How do you feel toward someone who blows his own horn? Why did the writer of Proverbs (27:2) say, "Let another man praise thee, and not thine own mouth"? What was Jesus teaching in his story about two men who prayed in the temple, one of them thanking God that he was superior to other men (Luke 18:9–14)? How do we as Christians look at those of other faiths? As Americans, how do we view other nations? What kind of attitude should we have toward others?

SEX EDUCATION

"The real question is not whether we shall have sex education —but what kind. *Playboy* magazine offers an installment every month that is seen by millions of kids. The motion picture industry has junked our minds with flesh and foolishness. And young people observe every day the attitudes of their parents, their neighbors, and their friends. Sex education is all around. . . . To deny this in the public sector would be a moral disaster."
—Dr. David Poling, quoted in *Christian Herald* magazine, December 1969.

Some sex education in the schools appears to be handled ignorantly or wrongly. But some we have seen in films and textbooks appears to us to be beautifully, reverently, and wholesomely presented. Is one misguided program reason for having none at all?

Many parents feel that sex education should be taught at home. But what if it isn't? What if the educators by default are television, the movies, the girlie magazines, the gutter? What is our responsibility toward our neighbors' children?

SEXUAL PROBLEMS: Don't Blame Them All on the Pilgrims!

Late in 1969, the noted anthropologist Ashley Montagu said on a television program that the Pilgrims had caused many of America's modern sexual hangups. The *Christian Century* pointed out in its issue of December 10 that Dr. Montagu, like many other slightly confused authorities, had mixed the Pilgrims up with the Puritans. It was the Puritans, not the Pilgrims, who passed all kinds of laws against the celebration of Christmas and various pleasures. Still, as the *Century* notes, the Puritans weren't so different from us as we sometimes think—for example, "long before the *Mayflower* sailed, in Mexico and other lands to the south of the New World, extension of the Spanish Inquisition was meting out harsh punishments for concubinage, bigamy and sodomy. As for sexual hangups, we don't like them either, Ashley. Nonetheless we suspect that extreme sexual permissiveness creates more hangups than it cures."

A number of medical and psychiatric experts have been telling us this lately; relaxing all the rules and regulations dealing with sex doesn't produce the heaven-on-earth some people thought it would, and in many cases seems to be creating hell-on-earth instead. Well put, *Christian Century!*

How many other problems or kinds of problems do we sometimes blame on the wrong people? Is there any easy answer to sexual problems, applicable equally to all? Should we expect easy answers if sex is as deep-rooted and pervasive as it appears to be? Do solutions lie in the direction of either rigid laws or complete permissiveness? Can God help our sexual hangups? How?

SHORTCUTS: "Horses Are for Courses"

Late in 1969, there was an unusual sight at a race track. One horse apparently became discouraged by its distance behind the front-runners, and jumped the fence to cut across the oval and catch up. But the sulky didn't quite make it, and a photograph in a sports magazine showed the horse halted by the vehicle: one wheel had cleared the fence, and one was still on the other side. Commented the magazine, "Horses are for courses—shortcuts not allowed."

Shortcuts are always appealing. Get-rich schemes, secrets of success in the stock market, easy routes to personality or power, mail-order degrees, even alleged "spiritual secrets" appeal to our hopes of avoiding the long struggles on the way to our goals. But in every realm success usually depends on patience, persistence, hard work, dogged determination; shortcuts usually leave the victim hung up one way or another, sooner or later.

The Bible and the great literature of mankind say little about shortcuts or success secrets, much about the elemental virtues of discipline, faith, zeal, hard work, patient endurance. Jesus promised his followers toil and troubles. He "for the joy that was set before him endured the cross"; his example and help admonish us to "run with patience the race that is set before us" (Hebrews 12:1, 2).

What shortcuts are most tempting to you? What is the best course through your most pressing problem? What options should not even be considered? Why?

See also SUCCESS.

SITUATION ETHICS AND THE GENERATION GAP

We usually think of the younger generation as the upholders of situation ethics and the new morality, and of the old standards and ideals as supported by the older members of society. At a press conference at the Minneapolis Congress of Evangelism,

September 10, 1969, Dr. Kenneth Chafin was asked a question about this, and he pointed out something else. In personal matters, Dr. Chafin said, young people are indeed often situationists, but in social matters they are absolute idealists. "The older generation reverses this," he went on. "Older people hold to absolute standards of personal morality in such matters as sexual conduct, but on the broader social scale—as regards business ethics, war, or indifference to the injustices of society against the poor and unfortunate—they may be very relativistic."

Is it true that we let situations alter cases in social matters, but not in personal ones? Is having a baby before marriage more immoral than burning babies alive with incendiary bombs? Is morality the possession of any one group or generation?

SOCIAL ACTION: A Christian Basic

"We do not stand to the United States the way Christians in Colossae or Philippi stood to Rome. Once we understand this, we will see that social action, far from being foreign to our faith, is basic to it."—Ernest T. Campbell.

Much has been said about the "social gospel." Is there such a thing? If so, what is it and how does it fit into the Christian faith?

SOCIAL ACTION: Both-And

"The church as a whole must be concerned with both evangelism and social action. It is not a case of either-or; it is both-and. Anything less is only a partial gospel, not the whole counsel of God."—Robert D. De Haan in *The Church Herald,* February 28, 1969.

Just before his 1969 evangelistic crusade in New York, Billy Graham said that there is no good reason why "in a city like

*this" people should live in slums when other people are driving
Cadillacs and living in magnificent dwellings. Do you agree?
Why, or why not?*

SOCIETY: Is It Sane?

Albert Szent-Gyorgi is a marine biologist who has given up
on the modern world. In an interview with Robert Reinhold in
the New York *Times* for February 20, 1970, he said the world
is governed by "idiots" under whose leadership one may observe
the inexorable destruction of the ocean, wildlife, even children.
He has written a book which appears to be his commentary on
another book about man called *The Naked Ape.* Dr. Szent-
Gyorgi's book is *The Crazy Ape.* Asking what kind of world
this is, he told Mr. Reinhold, "I say it is the nightmare of an
idiot."

R. D. Laing is a psychiatrist. In his books *The Divided Self*
and *Self and Others* he examines schizophrenia, that mental
malady in which the patient feels like an empty husk of nothing
in a universe that has no continuity, no future, no meaning.
Dr. Laing says that the schizophrenic's feelings of dread, apathy,
aloneness simply mirror our modern culture in which the individual is a number in a machine, in which technology is loosing
destructive forces against life, in which we are so often caught
up by forces of divisiveness and hate, cut off from one another,
left alone and uncared for. He quotes from such writers as
Samuel Beckett, Sören Kierkegaard, Franz Kafka and T. S.
Eliot in proof. Eliot's "hollow men," Beckett's pathetic creatures
of hopelessness, Kafka's antiheroes victimized by impersonal political forces, do suggest schizophrenic madness.

Dr. Laing believes that the person we call a schizophrenic
has learned what the world is like and in self-defense has
withdrawn into a sort of false self from which he observes,
detached, his own body. He also believes that there are false
selves who seem perfectly normal—the ideal wife, the model
child, the good student—who come to terms with the demands

put upon them by becoming something other than what they are. And he believes it may take a period of madness to discover sanity and thus overcome the mad world in which we live.

In *The Divided Self* Laing writes: "The statesmen of the world who boast and threaten that they have Doomsday weapons are far more dangerous, and far more estranged from 'reality,' than many of the people on whom the label 'psychotic' is fixed."

And in his book *The Social Contract* Robert Ardrey calls man "that creature mad beyond the craziest of hares, lunatic beyond all lemmings." He is writing somewhat facetiously about the difference between animals, who seem to know how to control excess population, and humans, who do not. Nevertheless, his statement is fundamentally serious.

Is man mad? Is our culture basically sane? Is it possible that our salvation, our sanity, is not within ourselves? Was Jeremiah correct when he wrote, "The heart is the most deceitful of all things, desperately sick" (17:9, NEB)? Can Christ heal a sick society? Can we help?

SONGS FOR NOW

Most of the songs in most hymn books are old, but at one time or another every single one was new. John Calvin and his fellow Protestants in Geneva set paraphrases of the Psalms to tavern tunes. General William Booth added religious words to the popular music of the nineteenth century, and asked, "Why should the devil have all the good tunes?"

Murray Neumeyer is an American with the same idea. He took the tune "Do Re Mi" from *The Sound of Music* and wrote these words[1]:

> Christ, the Lord, the Son of God;
> God, the one who sent Christ here;
> Here, the place we call the world;
> World, a home for you and me;
> Me, the self I long to know;

[1] Used by permission of the author.

Know, the quest of every man;
Man, the object of Christ's love . . .
So that brings us back to God.

Life, the aim of every man;
Free, a grant to all mankind;
Sin, the name of life gone wrong;
Grace, the yes of God to man;
Thanks, the yes of man to God;
Love, the greatest gift of all;
All, the circle of God's love . . .
So that brings us back to God.

Why, the quest of man's mind;
Why and what the source of life?
Why the evil and the good;
What the meaning of it all?
These and many more are they
Which perplex the human mind,
But behind it all we know
That there is a God of love.

Who am I and who are you?
What with you have I to do?
Who the architect of life?
Who the one beyond all truth?
God, the name of him who IS.
Christ, the name of him who came.
Man, the one for whom Christ died . . .
So that brings us back to God.

Christ, the Lord, the Son of God;
Christ, the God-man in our midst;
Christ, the one who seeks us out;
Christ, the one who paid the price;
Christ, incarnate, love divine;
Christ, the hope of all mankind;
Christ, the one who makes us whole:
Christ, the one who changes man.

Then there is the youth group of the Howard Memorial Presbyterian Church in Tarboro, North Carolina, who produced a musical entitled *Get Me to the World on Time,* with music adapted from *My Fair Lady.* In this musical parody the head of a church women's group sings, "All I want is a minister who can preach so that I can hear, good voice, good text, good cheer—oh, wouldn't that be loverly?" To this the women reply, "Lots of Scripture from him to me, words recited so Biblically, no thoughts politically!" Then they too ask whether that wouldn't be loverly.

In the same production two young people discover that black neighbors are moving to their street. "I have often felt they were dear to me," they sing, "but that was when they weren't quite so near to me"!

Why should a church or religious group of any kind stick to hymns mildewed with age? As other generations wrote their own songs and psalms, why shouldn't this one praise God and encourage and build up its members with its own words and music? We personally happen to believe that many of the old hymns are fine—but why should we be limited to the ancient, whether in church architecture, choir robes, ministerial garb, or the music of worship?

SPACE AND MAN

William Beebe was no armchair scholar. His extensive knowledge of nature was gained from explorations into the jungles of Asia and South America, and to the bottom of the ocean in the world's first bathysphere.

Beebe had much in common with his friend Theodore Roosevelt, who also loved nature and exploring. Often after a visit at Sagamore Hill, Beebe recalled, he and the President went outdoors to see who could first locate the Andromeda galaxy in the constellation of Pegasus. Then, gazing at the tiny smudge of distant starlight, either Beebe or Roosevelt would say:

"That is the spiral galaxy of Andromeda. It is as large as

our Milky Way. It is one of a hundred million galaxies. It is 750,000 light-years away. It consists of one hundred billion suns, each one larger than our sun."

After that thought had sunk in, Roosevelt used to flash his famous toothy grin: "Now I think we are small enough." And the two men would retire, put in their place in the limitless universe.

Does the size of the universe make God seem small—or does it reveal something of his greatness? Would the Bible writers be surprised by what we know today of space? (Consider Psalms 8 and 19, and Isaiah 40:12–17.) J. B. Phillips once asked some young people if they thought God understood relativity, and they said no. Does he? Do we need a measure of humility?

SPACE EXPLORATION: What Flag for Mars?

"Much as I would like to see the healing of historic religions, even more important for the world as a whole would be a reduction in personal and national selfishness as the ruling principle of our lives, and a steady increase in the practice of love and mutual trust. This would mean that whether the United States or the U.S.S.R. puts the first flag on Mars, the flag planted there would be a universal symbol—the flag of man, whose life has been made possible by God."[1]

It was thrilling to Americans to have the first flag on the moon, but if we should be the first to Mars, would it be more fitting to erect another American flag, or perhaps the flag of the United Nations? If a person has certain accomplishments, does he always have to keep boasting about them? If we carried the flag not of one country but of all earth to Mars, would other countries think less of us, or more?

Is it true that a nation as well as an individual may show

[1] Dr. Eugene Carson Blake, American church leader and General Secretary of the World Council of Churches, in *The Ladies' Home Journal*, December 1969.

signs of selfishness? Psychologists say that the person who is always trying to build himself up and belittle others is inwardly insecure. Could this be true of a whole country? Is it possible for a nation to practice trust and love? Which is better—that, or fear and hate?

SPACE EXPLORATION AND CHRISTMAS

Having reached the moon, man will doubtless, in time, explore Mars . . . Venus . . . the stars. Will anything be beyond our increasingly all-powerful grasp? Lona Fowler writes[1]:

> From the crests of the moon
> to the depths of the sea
> we know
> how to reach out.
>
> From Eden to Eternity
> we'll keep knowing
> how to spread disorder—
> lies and discord, spoilage, sorrow—
> we know the liberal arts of dying.
> But the space
> from one heart
> to another
> we know so little
> how to narrow.
>
> That space—requiring us
> to react within—
> is still the longest way to travel,
> the hardest goal to win.
>
> May the history and mystery of Christmas
> give us hope to keep on trying.

We do know how to reach out in miles and rockets. Do we know how to reach out to lonely, sorrowful hearts? Jesus did.

[1] Used by permission of the author.

206

*What can we learn from him about the most rewarding trip
of all, the exploration of another personality made in the image
of God?*

*How does Christmas give us hope? Isn't it easier to keep on
trying, now that we see how beautifully he did it in Galilee?*

STEWARDSHIP: The Golden Ladder

The medieval philosopher Maimonides was one of the wise
men of the ages. He once outlined the golden ladder of giving:

1. To give reluctantly, the gift of the hand, but not of the
   heart.
2. To give cheerfully, but not in proportion to need.
3. To give cheerfully and proportionately, but not until so-
   licited.
4. To give cheerfully, proportionately and unsolicited, but to
   put the gift into the poor man's hand, thus creating shame.
5. To give in such a way that the distressed may know their
   benefactor, without being known to him.
6. To know the objects of our bounty, but remain unknown
   to them.
7. To give so that the benefactor may not know those whom
   he has relieved, and they shall not know him.
8. To prevent poverty by teaching a trade, setting up a man
   in business, or in some other way preventing the need of
   charity.

*How far along this ladder do most people climb? Maimonides
stressed the individual poor man. Do organized charities and
philanthropic projects rob us of important contacts with individuals?*

STEWARDSHIP: Nature and the Golden Rule

"Animals have no souls; therefore, according to the most
authoritative Christian theologians, they may be treated as

though they were things. The truth, as we are now beginning to realize, is that even things ought not to be treated as *mere* things. They should be treated as though they were parts of a vast living organism. 'Do as you would be done by.' The Golden Rule applies to our dealings with nature no less than to our dealings with our fellow men. If we hope to be well treated by nature, we must stop talking about 'mere things' and start treating our planet with intelligence and consideration."—Aldous Huxley, "The Politics of Ecology," a paper of the Center for the Study of Democratic Institutions.

How responsible has mankind been in its treatment of Planet Earth? Should we apply the Golden Rule to "things" as well as people? Do we have a responsibility toward birds, animals, fields and forests, air and water? Can we survive unless we become good stewards of the only world we have?

For reference: Psalm 8; Genesis 1:28; 2:15; Numbers 14:21; Matthew 6:10; Luke 16:1–13.

See also POLLUTION AND US, YOUNG PEOPLE AND THE FUTURE.

STRESS FROM MODERN LIFE: Rats and the Rat Race

Dr. Joseph Buckley is a scientist who has been studying rats for eleven years and who has found that the present-day "rat race" is a term too close for comfort. Since 1959, according to a February 7, 1970, Associated Press report, Dr. Buckley has been subjecting thousands of rats to a stress chamber that simulates many of the conditions of modern city life: bright flashing lights, every kind of noise from buzzers to the roar of jet planes, and even a shaking, jostling motion similar to what you feel when you are riding to work in a car or train.

After a week of this, the rats develop permanent high blood pressure and become easily irritated and dangerous. Furthermore: "Exposed to the same stresses as the rats, the doctor and a graduate student began to notice a rise in their blood pressure, accompanied by increasing irritability."

Take an ordinary human being, put him in a ghetto filled not only with the kind of irritants Dr. Buckley has been studying, but thousands of other inconveniences that get steadily worse no matter how hard he tries to improve his environment, and don't let him out. Are you surprised if eventually something snaps and he wants to burn his ghetto down, or start planting bombs?

Through the worst part of the winter of 1970, at least one apartment house in the Bronx, New York, had no heat whatsoever and had had no water for two weeks, Murray Schumach reported in the February 8, 1970, New York *Times*. Families there found that no one did anything about their complaints and they had to go to bed wearing sweaters, mittens, socks, and sweat pants, and turn on their ovens to try to get warm. Some children got pneumonia while the tenants paid an average rent of $90 a month for their freezing, waterless apartments—in many of which the electricity had not worked for months.

Meanwhile the corporation which collects the rent is alive and well, and the tenants patiently walk down the street to a water hydrant to bring in water for their daily needs. How patient would you be in such a situation? How much would you take before you felt like starting a riot or a revolution? Is it surprising that sometimes people in areas like Watts or downtown Detroit or Newark riot—or that they don't riot more often? Are we our city brothers' keepers? If we can spend countless billions of dollars traveling to the moon and fighting in Vietnam, can we do something humane about our cities?

SUCCESS: How the Knicks Do It

The New York Knickerbockers were at the bottom of the national basketball heap when they acquired college basketball marvel Cazzie Russell. Even when they added another college miracle player, Bill Bradley, to their lineup, it was several years before the Knicks got far.

Then, in the 1969–70 season, the Knicks began winning game after game. How? "The defense is interrelated with the offense," said "Dollar Bill" Bradley, after the Knicks beat the Seattle Sonics. Lennie Wilkens, the Sonics' coach, said: "The thing that makes a team great is consistency, and the Knicks have consistency. We don't have any. The Knicks play well almost every night. They complement each other so well —they're great."

Not the stars but two simple techniques tell the Knicks' success story. One is *teamwork;* the other, *consistency.*

How does that apply to other things—like making your church effective? Can one person get far in any enterprise if his team-mates don't back him up?

How about being consistent? Is there much point in doing great one day if you fall flat the next?

Can you think of any real-life examples of these two things? Does Christ's choice of twelve disciples say anything about team-work and its importance? Does the Bible say anything about the value of consistency?

SUFFERING: Why?

As his dear wife lay dying of anoxia of the brain, Alan Paton pondered the incomprehensibility of suffering. The sit-uation would have been unendurable, Paton says in the book *For You Departed,* if he had not known of Francis of Assisi. That medieval man of God, coming upon some lepers, kissed the victims' sores, "believing as he did so that he was mediat-ing the love and pity of God."

Francis wrote later that "the Lord himself led me amongst them, and I showed mercy on them, and when I left them, what had seemed bitter to me was changed into sweetness of body and soul."

Why does God permit the horrible forms of suffering that fill the world? To give us an opportunity to show his incredible love and good will here on earth? To break the fascination for us of the visible world and to draw us to the permanent, the highest, the best—to himself?

For reference: Romans 8:18; II Corinthians 4:17; II Timothy 2:12; I Peter 4:19; I John 4:10–11.

THANKING GOD

The novel *Love Story* by Erich Segal (Harper) is the fast-moving account of the love and marriage of Oliver and Jenny. Before Jenny turns twenty-five, they discover that she is dying of leukemia.

Oliver says, "I began to think about God. . . . Not because I wanted to strike him on the face, to punch him out for what he was about to do. . . . No, the kind of religious thoughts I had were just the opposite. Like when I woke up in the morning and Jenny was still there. . . . I hoped there was a God I could say thank you to. Thank you for letting me wake up and see Jennifer."

Disaster may disintegrate faith, or begin it. Some of us easily forget God until we are caught in the middle of a storm. *When we do think of him, how often do we thank him for life, for the lives of our loved ones?*

The Christians of the first century were urged, ". . . let us continually offer praise as our sacrifice to God—the utterance of lips that glorify God's name. But do not forget to be helpful and generous, for this is the kind of sacrifice that pleases God" (Hebrews 13:15, 16, Goodspeed). Three things God likes us to be: thankful, helpful, generous!

THOUGHTLESSNESS: Practical Jokes

Pranksters in Shawnee, Oklahoma, took a stop sign away from a highway intersection and left it half a mile up the road. Chuckling as they drove off, they soon heard the results of their practical joke on the radio.

The Reverend Clifford L. Head, still in his thirties, was driving his station wagon, filled with the four other members of his family, past the intersection, when another car zoomed out of the warningless side road, directly into the front of the station wagon. Pastor Head was killed instantly. His wife had both arms and legs broken. She and the children and the other driver all had to be rushed to the hospital for emergency aid.

The practical joke turned out not to be very funny.

The incident above happened early in 1970. Some years earlier, certain workers in military defense plants discovered what fun air hoses could be. One jokester crept up to another man who was taking a nap near his locker during his lunch hour. The prankster tied the sleeping man's sleeves and cuffs tight, then "goosed" him with the tremendous air pressure in the hose. The pressure collapsed the victim's insides and killed him.

When is humor worthwhile and when is it destructive? Is it important to reflect about the possible consequences of things? Can verbal humor be destructive too? When, and how? Is thoughtlessness Christian?

TOMORROW: "Aquarius"

The popular song "Aquarius" says that we are at the drawing of a great new age, the Age of Aquarius, that will be marked by trust, understanding, love, harmony, and peace. According to the Hebrew Scriptures, there is such an age ahead. Isaiah the prophet described it in these terms:

"The spirit of the Lord shall rest upon him [the Messiah],
a spirit of wisdom and understanding,
a spirit of counsel and power,
a spirit of knowledge and the fear of the Lord. . . .
he shall judge the poor with justice . . .
Then the wolf shall live with the sheep,
and the leopard lie down with the kid;

the calf and the young lion shall grow up together,
and a little child shall lead them; . . .
They shall not hurt or destroy in all my holy mountain;
  for as the waters fill the sea
so shall the land be filled with the knowledge of the Lord."
(Isaiah 11:2, 4, 6, 9, NEB)

According to the New Testament, the Messiah who will
bring this about is the Christ, who must reign until his loving
will prevails and harmony fills the universe.

*How will the age of peace and love come about? What can
we do to help bring it? Is the Reign of Christ something
to sit back and wait for, or something to enter now, or both?*

See also THE FUTURE, PEACE, YOUNG PEOPLE AND THE FUTURE.

TOMORROW: When the Spring Snaps

We do not know who wrote this:

> This is the age
> of the half-read page
> and the quick hash
> and the mad dash
> the bright night
> with the nerves tight
> the plane hop
> with a brief stop
> the lamp tan
> in a short span
> the Big Shot
> in a good spot
> and the brain strain
> and the heart pain
> and the catnaps
> till the spring snaps
> and the fun's
> done.

But perhaps it sums up our age of speed-reading and anxiety, of moonshots and mushrooming numbers of people on an over-crowded planet, of fun and death.

What makes life worthwhile? When the heart stops, what then? Does your philosophy take into account the end? "Gospel" means "good news." Does your faith spell good news to you? Do you share it?

TROUBLE AND HOPE

Lord Caradon, the British envoy to the United Nations, knows how to put Christianity to work in times of trouble. Speaking at a luncheon held by the American Bible Society in May, 1969, he recalled the time when he had served as governor of Cyprus in the midst of a very troubled political situation. Knowing of his devout father's concern, the young governor was not surprised when he received a cable from England containing the words: "Two Corinthians: Eight, Nine." He knew the passage: "We are troubled on every side, yet not distressed; we are perplexed, but not in despair; persecuted, but not forsaken; cast down, but not destroyed."

It was a message of encouragement and assurance. Back to the anxious father went this cable: "Romans Five: Three, Four." The reply cable was a testimony of faith and hope: "And not only so, but we glory in tribulations also: knowing that tribulation worketh patience; and patience, experience; and experience, hope."

What do we do when trouble comes? Is there any better way to comfort someone with a problem than to give him the imperishable words of hope in Scripture? What do these passages indicate we can learn and profit from through shattering experiences?

TRUTH AND BUSINESS

Not everybody loves Arthur Godfrey. Like many radio and television personalities, he turns some listeners on and others off. From time to time, however, Arthur Godfrey takes a moral step anyone has to admire.

When he lost part of a lung from cancer in 1959, Godfrey decided to give up his contract to do Chesterfield commercials. It lost him, he says, more than two million dollars a year. Early in 1970, the New York *Times* reported on February 5, 1970, Godfrey was shocked to learn that the soap substitute he had been selling over the airwaves is a detergent—which he had been saying in his commercials it was not—and pollutes streams and lakes—which Godfrey says the maker told him it does not do. So he offered the manufacturers a choice: Either they would let him tell the truth about the detergent in future commercials, or he would have to stop. (Even though the detergent commercials pay more than the Chesterfield commercials did.)

Arthur Godfrey is probably in no danger of ending his days in the poorhouse. Money by the millions may not be as great a temptation to him as to you or me, but we don't know many people who would not be pleased with a larger pile of dollars, millions or otherwise.

Does anyone have to lie? What does a Christian do when he knows he is expected to bend, gloss over, or deny the truth? Is there a place for compromise? What do you think of Arthur Godfrey's action?

TRUTH AND TRUST: Communication vs. Secrecy

Ronald Ziegler is the man President Richard M. Nixon chose to be the White House Press Secretary, to keep the people informed through the newsmen about what is going on in the Administration.

"When Mr. Ziegler does provide information, reporters can't be sure it's right. First he said the President had not been involved in the Army's decision to drop the case against the Green Berets accused of murdering a Vietnamese secret agent; then the press secretary had to reverse himself. He so muddled the explanation of why Mr. Nixon had ordered a thirty-six-hour halt to B52 raids in South Vietnam that a senior White House official had to be called in to clarify.

"Two days before the President canceled November and December draft calls, the press secretary said suspension of the draft was not under consideration. A few days before Lewis Hershey was dropped as Selective Service Director, Mr. Ziegler said he had 'no information' to indicate Mr. Nixon was considering the move. Mr. Ziegler told the press that the President's meeting with Sir Robert Thompson was merely incidental to the British military authority's trip to Vietnam; later, Mr. Nixon told a nationwide TV audience that he had asked Sir Robert to make the fact-finding trip."[1]

Getting misinformation from the White House is not new, nor limited to the Administration of any one political party. But how can a democracy operate if the people don't know what their government is doing, or are told the opposite of the facts? Probably a government must keep some things secret, but some wonder whether this is for protection against a foreign enemy or for protection from the wrath of the people. And sometimes it seems that when a government finds itself involved in something embarrassing, its first reaction is to lie, almost automatically. Why?

Does a nation have a right to live by its own rules, invent its own morality? What happens when it is caught lying? Which is more important if you want people to believe you: an expensive propaganda machine, or a reputation for honesty and truthfulness?

Churches, too, sometimes cover up embarrassing facts. Is this good or bad? What increases trust and communication in a group more: the appearance of order and perfection, or admission of imperfection and confession of mistakes? What does the New Testament have to say about this? See, for example, James 5:16.

[1] John Pierson in *The Wall Street Journal*, December 28, 1969, p. 14.

TRUTH IN ADVERTISING

"We will install this new color television set in your home for only $25," says the advertisement. It does not add that you will then have to pay $50 a month for 18 months, or that if you are late on the last payment you may lose the set plus the $875 you have paid out previously.

Such ads are outlawed under the Truth in Lending law now in effect. Advertisers who mention one detail of credit, such as the easy down payment, have to state all the other relevant items—the number and amount of additional payments, for example. Companies who give credit must also state the finance charge and the annual rate of interest under this law.

It is often said that we cannot legislate morality. But we can and do legislate the things that make for a moral or immoral society. Truth hurts profits, sometimes, but laws requiring truth in business affairs prevent scoundrels from driving honest men out of business.

Christian legislators have been behind many laws such as Truth in Lending and Truth in Packaging. Why? Do Christians have a right to force their standards of right and wrong on other people? Do they have a right to sit by and let crime and wrongdoing get the upper hand?

See also BUSINESS AND ETHICS, TRUTH AND BUSINESS.

ULTIMATE REALITY

"The great Indian mystic Rabindranath Tagore once wrote a poem in which he compared our daily life to a narrow lane overhung with high buildings, between which there could be seen above a single strip of blue sky torn out of space. The lane, seeing the sun only for a few minutes at midday, asks herself—Is it real? Feeling some wayward breeze of spring wafted in from far-off fields, she asks—Is it real? But the dust and rubbish never rouse her to question. The noise of traffic, the jolting carts, the refuse, the smoke—these she accepts, these she concludes are clearly the real and actual things of life; and as for that strange strip of blue above, she soon ceases even to wonder about it, for so manifestly it is only a fancy, nothing real. This, says Tagore in effect, is precisely the truth about our ordinary mundane existence. The near things, the tangible, material things—these we accept, these we say are obviously the things that matter, they are solid, substantial fact: not recognizing that it is that streak of blue above, that fair glimpse of the spiritual, which is the essential reality for which every soul of man is made, and which alone gives meaning and perspective to all life's tasks and relationships."[1]

How often do we stop to look up?

UNDERSTANDING: Key to Peace?

Dr. Benjamin Spock is known to millions of Americans as the author of a best-selling book, *Baby and Child Care*. To millions more he is known as a militant crusader for peace—for he knows that war often destroys babies, and he is interested in seeking a world that will be safe for the babies he has helped reach maturity. In an interview with L. I. Stell[2] he thought out loud about man's aggression. The problem, he said, is not easy to solve. . . .

"The problem is man. Men take advantage of other men whenever they have the opportunity. I say the only slight hope of changing is for man to understand himself. Man has got to understand himself if he is to save himself.

". . . parents have got to bring up their children differently; bring them up to serve but also bring them up to be aware of the fact they are always trying to blame somebody else for their own faults. In addition, they've got to be taught an entirely different American history in school. You can't tell

[1] James S. Stewart, *The Wind of the Spirit* (Abingdon Press and Hodder and Stoughton, Ltd.). Used by permission.
[2] *Tempo*, December 1, 1970.

them America has always been glorious and that we've won our wars because God is on our side. You've got to teach them that some of our wars were disreputable, like the Spanish-American war. . . .

"Education has to be different all the way through. It is ridiculous to have psychology taught about the neuron and rats, for instance. The important thing is, 'What is man?' . . . We've got to teach endlessly the self-destructiveness of man. One: he is power-hungry. Two: Man's tendency toward self-deception. It is much more dangerous than the viciousness, the hostility of man. The murderousness of man is terrible. But much more dangerous is the fact that we have no idea of his murderousness, his hostility, and the fact that he is always calling his own hostility somebody's else hostility, which is—as an externalized example—the international situation between the United States and North Vietnam. . . .

"Man can only save himself by understanding himself better, yet I'm haunted by the question of whether he can be taught to understand himself better. Or, even if he is taught to understand himself better, whether this will ever stand up when the crises come."

Do you agree that understanding is a crucial key to peace and order among men? Is it true that human beings often deceive themselves about their own motives, their hostility and fear? Is Dr. Spock's conclusion too pessimistic? Can man save himself?

UNDERSTANDING THE YOUNG

"I am so afraid that when I am forty, my daughter will have for a father a man who does not understand, who does not listen and who does not learn from her. She may have for a father a man who unconsciously sold his idealism and commitment for the security of a bank account, a home and a little comfort. . . . Her father may be a man whose bitterness is so pervasive that he will be loath to see her generation succeed where his failed."[1]

Not many adults are as sensitive to the needs and moods of the young as Julius Lester, the brilliant black revolutionary. We may not agree with his radical philosophy, but we can all appreciate his desire to keep in touch with the way young people think, not only to understand them but also to listen to them and learn from them!

Do young people have a corresponding duty to try to understand their elders, listen to and learn from them? Who is most responsible for the generation gap: the young or the old? How can we guard against the cynicism and bitterness that often seem to accompany age?

See also YOUNG PEOPLE, ALIENATION OF YOUTH.

UNEMPLOYMENT: Is It Acceptable?

In 1969 nearly three million people were unemployed; and as 1970 began, the number was steadily rising while the federal government indicated that a further increase was "acceptable." It was not acceptable, we think, to the thousands of men and women being turned out of their jobs every month, nor to those who are usually the last to be hired and the first fired.

While approximately one American in ten is black, one in five—twice the proportion—is unemployed. While 12 percent of our teen-agers are without jobs, 21 percent of black teen-agers are. While 3 percent of the unemployed are white women, more than 7 percent are black women.

More black persons are now being accepted in good colleges and considered for good jobs. To the Christian and to the American who really believes in liberty and justice for all, this is great news. But there are still far too many schools where black students are not welcome, far too many companies where

[1] Julius Lester, "Reflection on Reaching the Age of Thirty," *Katallagete,* Fall 1969.

white employees are preferred, far too many neighborhoods where a Negro family cannot buy a home.

Can't we do better than this? Is it acceptable to you to have three million people out of work, six hundred thousand of them the "wrong" color? Would I be patient and forgiving if the depth of my tan made a difference in what I could earn, where I could live?

UNITY IN THE CHURCH

"How really important is it whether we use fermented wine or grape juice at the communion table, whether we dot all the i's and cross all the t's in our statements of faith, or even how basically important is it who lays hands on whom? When God lays his hands on men and women it doesn't make much difference what church they belong to, or perhaps whether they belong to any church at all."[1]

Do we have to agree on everything before we can acknowledge that our fellow Christians are our brothers and sisters? How important are creeds, sacraments, and ordination? Are they more important than faith and love?

For reference: Acts 10:1-35; Ephesians 2:11-22; 4:1-7.

See also BROTHERHOOD, CHURCH.

VIOLENCE: Is It Addictive?

What happens when a youngster watches shootings, lynchings, burnings, and other forms of violence and torture hour after hour after hour—as the average American child does on television and in many motion pictures? For years there has been a heated debate between those who viewed the effects of tele-

[1] Howard L. Trueman in *The United Church Observer*, October 15, 1969. Used by permission.

vision with alarm, afraid it would corrupt the child-viewers, and those who felt it was harmless or even beneficial.

One man who has some solid facts on this subject is Dr. Victor B. Cline, a psychologist at the University of Utah who has performed some relevant laboratory experiments. Fastening wires to the arms, noses, and other parts of the bodies of children who viewed specific TV programs, he studied the rate their heartbeats increased the first time they saw violent episodes—and the decreasing rate as violence became an old story. Some of Dr. Cline's conclusions were reported in *Life* for January 30, 1970. Among them:

1. Many children are already desensitized by the amount of violence they see regularly in the hours (an average of fifteen to twenty per week) they spend viewing television. Violence has become an accepted, almost normal part of their lives.

2. Such acts of violence may be imitated when the child grows up. Dr. Cline says, "I am convinced that any U.S. soldiers who shot down Vietnamese women and children at My Lai had been desensitized."

3. The amount of television watching a child does should be limited. Dr. Cline's own children are not permitted more than one hour of viewing a week.

4. Violence in excess as well as pornography should be reason for withholding the "G" rating from motion pictures. In other words, we should accept the fact that teaching a child unnatural acts of destruction and inhumanity is as much a perversion as exposing him to raw sex.

Does it matter what we fill our minds with? Is violence on the entertainment screen something for the government to regulate, for the producers themselves to control, or for parents to handle? What does the Bible say about the meaning and effects of violence? Compare Genesis 6:11; Proverbs 4:14–19; Amos 1; Romans 12:14–21.

Is it true that we, too, may become desensitized to violence, cruelty, starvation, mass murder through repeated exposure to it on television, the radio, and the pages of our newspapers? What can we do to keep Christ-sensitive hearts and minds?

222

Do you agree with Dr. Victor Cline's conclusions about television and motion pictures? What additional suggestions might be offered parents? Is it good for children to go to the movies regularly no matter what kind of picture is being shown? Does your community adequately police its entertainment— excluding corrupting films and enforcing age regulations?

WAR: "The Spirit of Kill"

"We've got to teach these men to be mean, they must look mean, act mean, because they are going against a dirty enemy, an enemy that recognizes no sportsmanship, but who uses every means in his power to kill—in order to combat that spirit we've got to make our men just a little bit more proficient in the art of killing than they are, we've got to put the spirit of kill in our men, and so put the fear of Christ in the Germans. . . ."[1]

As a war progresses, each side seems compelled to tell its men that the other side is so unfair, so brutish that *we* must be dirtier and more brutal than they are if we are to win. And what the war is all about is: Kill. Search and destroy, run up the kill count, nail that coonskin to the wall, get him before he gets you. So otherwise decent young men are filled with the spirit of kill, and even Christ becomes another tool in the propaganda arsenal of the war machine.

How is the name of the Lord taken in vain? Is Christ someone whose "fear" is promoted by killing off our enemies?

WAR: The War Prayer

Dan Beard, founder of the Boy Scouts of America, was a naturalist who illustrated a number of the books of his friend Mark Twain. During one of his visits with Twain, the humorist

[1] Major Reginald Barlow, 302nd Infantry, Camp Devons, Massachusetts, September 28, 1917, as quoted in *The Outlook,* October 10, 1917.

read a new piece of writing entitled "The War Prayer." "Everyone who has heard it so far," said Twain, "tells me I must not let it be published. They say that people would call it a sacrilege."

"Still," said Beard, "you are going to publish it, are you not?"

Twain shook his head. He said he had told the truth in "The War Prayer," and the only people in this world who can tell the truth are the dead. "It can be published after I am dead."

It was, but little was heard of this remarkable work until Harper & Row published it recently in book form.

"The War Prayer" begins with the excitement of a country that has just become involved in war. Flags are flying, patriotic speeches are being made everywhere, and in a certain church the minister makes a very patriotic prayer. He asks the protection of God on the young men in the armed forces, victory on the war fronts, and defeat for the enemy.

During the pastoral prayer an old man wearing a long robe and long white hair walks slowly up the aisle, and as the startled minister concludes his prayer, touches him on the arm and takes his place in the pulpit with the words, "I come from the Throne—bearing a message from Almighty God!"

The amazed congregation listens as the stranger with the burning eyes explains what the pastoral prayer really means. Beseeching God for victory in the war, he says, really means, "Help us to tear their soldiers to bloody shreds." It means, "Blast their homes, send their wives and children out into the snow with bleeding wounds, utterly destroy them." The stranger asks the congregation if this is what they truly desire.

"The War Prayer" concludes, "It was believed afterward that the man was a lunatic, because there was no sense in what he said."

Was *there any sense in the stranger's words? Does it make sense in the name of friendship or honor or whatever to burn villages and babies, rip apart the bodies of civilians with bombs*

*that explode into thousands of fragments designed to kill every-
thing they touch, poison crops, destroy everything that grows
in an area, and blast it into a condition more lifeless than
the surface of the moon? Is bombing and bulldozing villages
out of existence and sending the men into graves, the mothers
into barbed-wire "pacification areas," and the daughters into
prostitution, the way to win the respect of a people we say
we have come to defend? Can there be anything just or honorable about the way war is waged today?*

WAR: What Is It Doing to Our Boys?

Those who question the wisdom of such military adventures
as the war in Southeast Asia are often opposed by others who
urge them to "support our boys." But one reason so many
people oppose the war is precisely because they *do* "support our
boys." They are concerned not only over the senseless destruction of life in Asia but also over what this is doing to the youth
in uniform.

The United States Senate has long been concerned with such
matters. The Washington *Post* for January 28, 1970, reported
the testimony given before a Senate subcommittee by Dr. Robert
Jay Lifton, a former Air Force psychiatrist now at Yale University. He said that the current war is producing a "very large
pool of young, embittered" veterans who are forced to experience "a combination of profound inner confusion, helplessness
and terror. . . . fear, rage and frustrations mount."

Seeing their buddies killed, said Dr. Lifton, the GIs come to
regard all Vietnamese as enemies (forgetting that it is the
Vietnamese we are supposed to be defending!) and easily succumb to such "psychic numbing" and "general brutalization"
that it becomes easy to gun down even old men, mothers, and
babies. He reported that the veterans he knew were not surprised at reports of the My Lai massacre: "Virtually all of
them had either witnessed or heard of similar incidents."

What happens to veterans of the Vietnam War? Dr. Lifton

said many of them will sooner or later experience, as a result of their experiences, psychiatric problems ranging all the way from depression to severe psychoses. He predicted that many will refuse to talk or even think about the war, will be psychologically numbed, and will take night jobs. One veteran told Dr. Lifton, "I couldn't stand looking at those nine-to-five people who sent me to Vietnam."

Americans who desire peace do indeed support the boys in Southeast Asia—support their right to life, their right to a guilt-free existence, their right to two arms and two legs apiece, their right to health of mind and body. *What is more important than these?*

WAR AND BODY COUNTS

One of the things about the Vietnam War that has long bothered many Americans is the military emphasis on "body counts" and "kill ratios" and "search and destroy missions." Is the purpose of the war to see how many people we can kill? How does that differ from Hitler's purpose in his war?

Henry B. Rothblatt, Esq., is a prominent New York lawyer who defended the Green Berets when they were charged with assassinating a Vietnamese, and who in 1970 defended First Lieutenant James B. Duffy, charged by the Army with killing another Vietnamese, a prisoner. Mr. Rothblatt said that Lieutenant Duffy's division had orders not to take prisoners, that prisoners were killed because the division needed high body counts to show how effective it was. He said the "whole body count business" precipitated "whatever occurred." He stated that "officers feel the only way to test the efficiency of their units is by the number of bodies they pile up." So Daniel Southerland quotes him in the February 14, 1970, *Christian Science Monitor*.

Other reports from Vietnam indicate that sometimes food, passes, and even water were withheld from American soldiers until they made their "kill."

All this strikes some citizens as a fiendish way to carry on a war. Are we supposed to "win the hearts and minds of the people of Vietnam" by killing them off in the hundreds of thousands? Has our government encouraged the murder of war prisoners? If this is a part of war, do we need a new look at war itself?

WAR AND THE CHURCH

"A church that is not able to take a firm stand against war," said theologian Harvey Cox recently, ". . . is not a church which deserves to be believed."

Do you agree or disagree? Should the church oppose all wars, support all wars, or discriminate (if it can) between wars that seem just and those that don't? During World War I it was sometimes intimated in American churches that if Christ were on earth he would carry a bayonet against the Germans. Is such a Christ the Christ of the New Testament? What should our attitude be toward modern war with its weapons of mass extermination? Is war today basically any different from war in ancient times, or not?

WAR AND THE CHURCH: Blessings on Order?

"The churches of practically every description can be relied upon to bless a popular war, and to see in it an opportunity for the triumph of whatever godly design they choose to further. Some care must, of course, be exercised to facilitate the transition from the condemnation of wars in general, which is a traditional attitude on the part of the Christian sects, to the praise of a particular war. This may be expedited by securing suitable interpretations of the war very early in the conflict by conspicuous clericals; the lesser lights twinkle after."[1]

How much truth is in these cynical statements? The churches of different areas can sing, "We are not divided; all one body

[1] Harold D. Lasswell in *Propaganda Technique in the World War*, p. 73.

we" until wartime, when each church backs whatever country or territory it happens to be in. There are of course notable exceptions. Witness the courageous opposition to Nazism of the Confessing Church of Germany in World War II, and the forthright stand against the war in Vietnam by many American churches and synagogues and their members.

Is a church something to be used to further whatever causes the masters of propaganda choose? Should it "bless" any war? If it should rally behind a particular war, should it be careful to investigate what it is doing, to learn whether someone is cynically using it?

WAR AND THE CHURCH: An Eye for an Eye?

During World War I a physical director of the YMCA supplied American soldiers with a manual entitled *Hand-to-Hand Fighting*. The manual listed the various parts of the enemy's anatomy the soldier was expected to know how to obliterate, as:

"*Eyes*. Never miss an opportunity to destroy the eyes of the enemy. In all head holds use the finger on the eyes. They are the most delicate points in the body and easy to reach. The eye can easily be removed with the finger."

This choice information is recounted in the book *Preachers Present Arms: The Updated Record* by Dr. Ray H. Abrams, a sociology professor at the University of Pennsylvania, published by Herald Press. Dr. Abrams' unbiased, painstaking survey of war and the church notes the overwhelming approval of a majority of clergymen not only of World War I but also of hand grenades and bayonets. He quotes a wartime editorial by Albert C. Dieffenbach, editor of the Unitarian *Christian Register,* stating what Dieffenbach believed Jesus would do: "He would take bayonet and grenade and bomb and rifle and do the work of deadliness against that which is the most deadly enemy of his Father's kingdom in a thousand years. . . ." (What superlatives war fever brings forth!)

Dr. Abrams also quotes a book called *The Practice of Friend-*

ship, published under the guidance of the YMCA by George Stewart and Henry Wright. Designed to "Christianize every phase of a righteous war," it encourages the young soldier not to slacken at bayonet drill, "when men charge over the embankment and into a trench to drive their bayonets into straw dummies made to imitate human bodies with wooden frames inside to represent bones." The writer (apparently Stewart) says he could not do this until he could see Jesus himself running a bayonet through an enemy's insides, but that he was granted such a heavenly vision of his Lord at work against the hated Hun, and from "the thickest of the fight" he heard Jesus say, "Lo, I am with you alway, even unto the end." His vision of Jesus holding a bayonet produced "peace and power I had never known before."

The Puritans praised God after burning an Indian village and destroying everyone inside, young or old. Is this the kind of religion for which Christ died? It is precisely because he substituted life for murder, truth for lies, love for hate that he has won the ages' admiration. The iniquity of trying to use him to sanctify war is that it makes him into the exact opposite of all he was and stood for.

Is there such a thing as Christian morale in wartime? Is there a Christian answer to war? Does bombing and bayoneting people win us friends, influence, or any lasting good?

See also INFLATION, PEACE.

WELFARE: What Is It Like?

Just suppose for a moment you are a mother whose husband drank excessively and finally left you. You have seven children —you were once a Catholic—and you have always worked. But the children's needs finally put you on welfare, from which you get about $70 a month for clothing, your rent, and $283 for food. If you earn more than $25 a month, the government deducts the amount from your welfare payments.

Living that way is not easy, Mrs. Jean Davis (not her real

name) told Shirley Hunter. "My kids always seem to be hungry," she was quoted in the *Western Catholic Reporter* for January 18, 1970. Even though she stretches her food money with macaroni, spaghetti, and soup bones, and buys the cheapest meat available, Jean finds it's impossible to have meat every day. "And even by mixing fresh milk and powdered milk, there's no way I can give them all the milk they should be getting."

This mother wishes she could give some of her children music lessons. "There's no way I can help them develop their talents. I wish there was some way that kids didn't have to be held back through no fault of their own."

Perhaps the image of the person on welfare would change if we could meet Jean Davis and her family. Should her children be culturally deprived and physically and mentally stunted from malnutrition because their father deserted them? Should society keep them on the under side of grinding need?

What is welfare really like? In 1969 there were families throughout America who tried to find out by living on a welfare diet for a week. They learned what it was like to try to buy enough food for their families on the amount of money a welfare family gets. All of them finished the week with a cry of thanksgiving that they didn't have to continue, and a new sense of what it means to be poor.

Would we sympathize with the poor more if we did that? Would we condemn all welfare recipients as "loafers" if we personally knew some of the widows, deserted mothers, cripples, and the many others who cannot do the kind of work you and I do? Would it be worth a church's while for its members to become well acquainted with some people on welfare? Should a Christian look down on someone who for one reason or another must ask for charity?

WISDOM VS. INTELLIGENCE

In January 1970, Max Born died. A close friend of Albert Einstein and a colleague of Max Planck and Otto Hahn, the nuclear physicists, he was one of the great minds of the twentieth century. In an interview on German television before his death, Born commented: "I'd be happier if we had scientists with less brains and more wisdom."

Max Born was concerned about the misuse of scientific discoveries. To survive in the 1930s he had to flee from Nazi Germany. In 1957, he took part with other scientists in the Göttingen Manifesto against nuclear weapons. Germany's President Heinemann wrote his widow that Born had tried "to hold a mirror up to his fellows and warn his colleagues against following the wrong paths."

The supply of human brainpower today seems almost infinite. Whether the objective is exploring space or inventing a weapon that will kill more people quicker, science can come up with a solution. What we need is not brains but wisdom.

What is wisdom? Would you agree that it is "the right use of knowledge"? What does the Bible say about wisdom? See Psalm 111:10; Proverbs 3:17, 18, 35; 8:11, 34; James 1:5. Do scientists have an obligation for the right use of what they discover? What kind of world would we have if no researcher, businessman, or worker felt any moral duty to God or his fellow men? Is such a lack what is most wrong with our age?

WITNESSING: Live!

"Jesus says: 'Live! Let the light of your life—the manifestation of God at work in the painful, practical, personal areas of life—shine!' We ought to be living such a radiant life that it prompts the question, 'Why are you the way you are?' and opens the way for a positive answer of what God has done. There's nothing more silly than the answer to an unasked question. That's witnessing of the lowest order. But there's nothing more powerful and contagious than the answer to a sincere question about the source of our quality of life. That's witnessing of the highest order."[1]

[1] Lloyd John Ogilvie, *A Life Full of Surprises*. Word Books, p. 67.

When Christians try to witness, what answers do they sometimes give to questions that are not asked? What are the needs many people do have? Then, what are they really asking us for? Do we have the answers? Where can we get them?

WORK, PRAYER, FUN

The world-renowned poet W. H. Auden talked about life in its fullness when he came to New York in February 1970. He said there are three essentials to the full life: work, prayer, and carnival. The first two are fairly self-explanatory. By "carnival," Auden apparently means something like the New Orleans carnival gala, the Mardi Gras, in which people can get together and celebrate their unity in poking fun at the grotesque, the exaggerated, while fears lose their hold. We wonder whether reading a favorite comic strip, watching a humorous television program, or simply exchanging jokes with a neighbor may not serve the same purpose: learning to relax through fun and good humor.

Jesus was a worker. For thirty years he learned and practiced carpentry, and then in three he built the Church. He was a man of prayer; sometimes he prayed all night. And he was a person of great good humor. There is tremendous wit in some of his illustrations, like the word-picture he painted of the man who was careful to keep every insect out of the cup from which he drank, only to swallow a whole ungainly camel. Our Lord apparently enjoyed life to the full.

Work—doing something well that we enjoy doing and that contributes to the world's good: that is important. Prayer—bringing our needs and those of the people around us before God, and enjoying his presence: that is vital. Fun—learning to relax, laugh, enjoy the humor of life: that is indispensable to survival. Yes, these three forms of activity are necessary for the life that is full and free.

As machines become able to do more and more of the work of humans, will work remain important? Shorter working hours

mean more leisure time. Does it matter how such time is spent?
Fun is important. What happens when it is enjoyed at the
expense of someone else? What would you say are the five
most important things in life?

WORSHIP: Church and Hypocrisy

[Even though men meet together in worship:] "The final
breakthrough to fellowship does not occur, because, though
they have fellowship with one another as believers and as devout
people, they do not have fellowship as the undevout, as sinners.
The pious fellowship permits no one to be a sinner. So everybody must conceal his sin from himself and from the fellowship.
. . . Many Christians are unthinkably horrified when a real
sinner is suddenly discovered among the righteous. So we remain
alone with our sin, living in lies and hypocrisy."[1]
Is that true of your church? What can you do about it?

See also HONESTY, PRAYER.

WORSHIP: Going Anywhere?

Day after day, day after day,
We struck nor breath nor motion,
As idle as a painted ship
Upon a painted ocean.

Week after week, week after week,
We worshiped without fail.
Yet never did our souls invoke
The Wind upon our sail.[2]

[1] Dietrich Bonhoeffer, quoted in *Buried Alive* by Paul G. Johnson (John
Knox Press).
[2] *Stains on Glass Windows* by Ken Anderson (Word Books). Used by permission of the publisher.

A friend tells me he has pictured church life as a space exploration society which meets in a rocket. Every Sunday morning everyone gets into the rocket, the fuel is tested, there is a lecture on space travel . . . and then everyone gets out and goes home until the whole thing is repeated next Sunday. But the rocket never gets off the ground.

What is worship? Should it (or the worshipers) be going somewhere? In most activities there is either progress or stagnation. Is there "progress" in worship? Is such progress measurable?

Have we forgotten the Wind for our sails?

See also CHURCH, HOLY SPIRIT.

WORSHIP AND ACTION

"Most people think of the church as a drama," Dr. James Kennedy said recently, "with the minister as the chief actor, God as the prompter, and the laity as the critic. What is actually the case is that the congregation is the chief actor, the minister is the prompter, and God is the critic."

What if Sunday morning worship were not a beautiful drama for our pleasure but a place to get instructions for our own week-long service of God? What if it mattered less whether the minister repeated himself than whether we repeated his words in our day-to-day life? What if we stopped criticizing one another while we concentrated on living in the presence of God?

YOUNG PEOPLE: Coexisting with Them[1]

"For some time now I have been compiling my own secret set of rules on How to Survive and Be Happy Though Sur-

[1] The following excerpt is by Landrum R. Bolling, President of Earlham College. It appeared in the Fall 1969 *Earlhamite* and is reprinted by permission.

rounded by College Students. I pass them on . . . not as an infallible guide, but as a set of suggestions for the preservation of civility and sanity. Here they are:

"1. LISTEN. You won't learn much from young people if you do all the talking. You'll be surprised at how much sense they talk, however senseless they may look.

"2. KEEP SMILING. A large percentage of us of the older generation unconsciously or deliberately glare, sneer or frown when we look at college students. Most of them are remarkably perceptive; they know when we're hostile. It is difficult for most people, young or old, to communicate with others who are clearly antagonistic.

"3. DON'T ASK THEM WHY THEY LOOK THE WAY THEY DO. If they can't explain it to their parents, they can't explain it to you. Anyway, they don't really know.

"4. DON'T TELL THEM HOW HARD AND HOW JOYFULLY YOU WORKED IN YOUR YOUTH. Theirs is a different world; they have no conception of the world through which we lived in the Depression and in World War II and little curiosity to learn about it. Sad or wrong, but it's true.

"5. LEVEL WITH THEM. They are amazingly open and honest, if you approach them in a spirit of openness and honesty. And there's little or nothing you can't talk about.

"6. DON'T TRY TO BE ONE OF THEM. Among the most pathetic creatures over thirty are those synthetic adolescents who try to dress, talk, act and look like college students. Oh, there's an occasional middle-aged folksinger who can get away with it. Most of the rest of us, on or off the campus, can't.

"7. SHARE WITH THEM YOUR OWN HIGHEST HOPES AND FINEST PURPOSES. It will surprise and delight them to discover that plenty of old people are idealists too. They have been fed too much nonsense about the lack of social purpose among their elders.

"8. BELIEVE IN THEM. They'll sense it when you do. And, as in all generations, they will respond, eventually, to that belief."

You can read the good humor between these lines, but there is much deep seriousness and sense to President Bolling's words —and we believe they might be applied very well to young people in our high schools, churches, communities, and homes.

What are young people looking for, anyway? Is it possible that they are searching for the finest things of life even more diligently and seriously than we are trying to convince them to look for these things? Do we have something to offer them consistent with their high expectations?

YOUNG PEOPLE: Is Discipline What They Need?

"Linda failed to return home from a dance Friday night. On Saturday she admitted she had spent the night with an Air Force lieutenant.

"The Aults decided on a punishment that would 'wake Linda up.' They ordered her to shoot the dog she had owned about two years. On Sunday, the Aults and Linda took the dog into the desert near their home. They had the girl dig a shallow grave. Then Mrs. Ault grasped the dog between her hands and Mr. Ault gave his daughter a .22-caliber pistol and told her to shoot the dog.

"Instead, the girl put the pistol to her right temple and shot herself.

"The police said there were no charges that could be filed against the parents except possibly cruelty to animals."[1]

Probably Linda's parents meant well. They were understandably shocked by their daughter's behavior, and they decided on a punishment they thought would be effective. No doubt they did not dream what would happen as a result.

Is discipline the main thing young people need today? Is there a time when punishment is too late? What do children and young people need most from the older generation?

[1] The New York *Times,* February 7, 1968.

236

YOUNG PEOPLE AND CHRIST: Popular Songs

Some popular songs are atrociously bad, but some are surprisingly worth listening to—carefully. Peter, Paul, and Mary have a song entitled "Tramp on the Street" that begins, "Jesus, he died on Calvary's tree" and refers to the nails in his hands and feet and says he shed his blood "for you and for me." The song "Superstar" is addressed to Jesus Christ. The title of another song is "Jesus Is a Soul Man."

Most young people today do not seem attracted by formal religion, but many of them are fascinated by Jesus and are looking for what he stood for and stands for and offers. They may not be singing the old hymns, but some of them are creating new hymns to the One who was executed in his early thirties.

Furthermore, many of their songs present important religious truths even though they do not use religious language. "Everyday People," for example, speaks of the blue person who can't accept the green one, the rich one that will not help the poor one, but, "We got to live together."

What are young people looking for today? Are their desires all wrong, all good, or both? If Christ came to earth today as he came two thousand years ago, what group do you think would most turn against him? What group would most accept him? What in him appeals to young people? How can a church show this to youth? Or can it?

YOUNG PEOPLE AND THE CHURCH

"The church has lost the young adult generation," Methodist lay evangelist Harry Denman said recently. R. Eugene Crow was quoted by the American Baptist News Service as giving four reasons why we lose young people.

1. Youth "have been reared on scientific concepts," and what is said to them has either to be put in scientific terms or related to what they know of the universe.

2. Young people "are interested in a challenge, not in comfort." Many of them have little interest in making money but will go to the ends of the earth, via Vista, the Peace Corps, or anything else, to share knowledge and know-how with the less fortunate.

3. Youth today want to know "how the gospel applies to the great social issues of our time. At the same time they continue to be interested in how it applies to the private, personal areas of life."

4. Young people are geared to participation and involvement in education, whether by way of school or television, and want "significant opportunities for discussion and action."

What is wrong with these desires? Should we be asking, What is wrong with a church that does not try to meet these desires on youth's terms? What is actually more ready-made for young people's grasp than Christianity with its infinite Creator, its gospel of challenge for both social and private life, its demand for action? How soon will we appreciate the tremendous validity in what our young people demand?

YOUNG PEOPLE AND COMMUNICATION: How Do You Talk to Teen-agers?

"They won't talk to us," many parents say of their teen-age youngsters. But the trouble is not always on the young people's side. The generation gap can be bridged. In *Parent–Teen-ager Communication,* an excellent Public Affairs Pamphlet published at 381 Park Avenue, New York 10016, Millard J. Bienvenu, Sr., suggests some important guidelines:

1. *Learn to listen.* (Some parents talk but never hear what their children are saying.)

2. *Find a time to talk when young people want it.* Don't miss these opportunities.

3. *Hear the adolescent out without interrupting his conversation.*

4. *Try to listen calmly.*

238

5. *Avoid being judgmental.* "It is not necessary, nor advisable, to condone a youngster's attitude or habits, but it is important to accept his feelings about what he does."

6. *Learn to listen "between the lines."* Your child may be trying to tell you more than he is actually putting into words.

7. *Permit expression of feeling.* No two individuals see everything exactly alike, and young people have to learn to form their own feelings and opinions without being castigated.

8. *Avoid barriers to self-expression.* Don't do anything that will keep your teen-ager from confiding in you as completely as possible.

9. *Develop a courteous tone of voice in communication.*

10. *Hold a family conference.*

(Above material in italics or quotation marks copyright © 1969 by Millard J. Bienvenu, Sr.)

When Jesus was only twelve, his parents took him on an eighty-mile trip—requiring many days away from home—and were so relaxed about where he was that when he stayed behind, on the return trip, it was three days before they started looking for him (Luke 2:41–52). Some parents are probably too permissive, others too rigid; blessed is the teen-ager whose father and mother are sure of themselves and willing to let their children develop into the pattern God has implanted in each.

Do you agree with Mr. Bienvenu's suggestions about communication? Is there really a generation gap? What in your own adolescence is of value to you now in your relations to teenagers?

YOUNG PEOPLE AND DISCRIMINATION

Suppose you were a seventeen-year-old girl who had just won your city's beauty contest. Judi Belk is and did. Late in 1969 she won the title "Miss Teen-age Alexandria," and was given a trip to Dallas to represent her Virginia city there in the Miss Teen-age America contest. As she talked to the other contestants, Judi realized that something seemed wrong.

Other contestants had received various honors from their cities. Several girls had received a key to the city; one had been escorted by the governor of her state. So far as the officials of Alexandria (a gracious city close to Washington, D.C.) were concerned, Judi's award might never have been given. Neither the Governor nor the Mayor nor anyone else gave her any kind of official recognition.

If you were Judi, wouldn't you think something was odd about this? Do you suppose it might have anything to do with the fact that Judi is the first Negro ever to win the title of Miss Teen-age Alexandria, and the only Negro to compete last November at Dallas? "I don't want to go out on a wall and say it's because I'm black," said Judi, one of whose main interests in life is improving race relations, "but I think that's about it."

By the time this is published, let us hope that what seems like a grave discourtesy has been amended. Surely a city as great as Alexandria has nothing to fear from as lovely and intelligent a teen-ager as Miss Belk. But let us look at our own communities and attitudes. *How often are young people discriminated against in your town—because they are young? Or because they are the "wrong" color? Or because they come from the "wrong" part of town? Or because they don't have "the right connections"?*

Jesus was barely past thirty when he was killed by the religious and political establishment he had angered—and most of his apostles, if not all, were probably quite young when he chose them. Youth can do a lot for the world if it has a fraction of a chance.

YOUNG PEOPLE AND FUN: "The Pleasure Seekers' Club"

In October 1969, *Together* magazine published a letter[1] from an angry young man who said that young people today

[1] Reprinted from *Together* magazine, January 1970. Copyright © 1969 by The Methodist Publishing House.

want "love, not war—kindness, not hate—freedom, not endless rules—drugs, not jail—sex, not a marriage certificate." He said that mankind is suffering while God is off somewhere in the distance, and he wrote glowingly of his "Pleasure Seekers' Club," whose only rule, apparently, is to have fun. Three months later, *Together* published a number of letters in response. This one from a sixteen-year-old girl said some things we think are worth reprinting and pondering.

"I dated and ran around since I was about thirteen. I had sex with five or six different steadies. I dated two guys who tried drugs. I know what the 'in scene' is. But as far as I'm concerned, it's out.

"I have moved frequently and have never really been in any special clique or school, or anywhere. My whole life seemed useless and a mess.

"Six months ago I met a guy who really has something going. He has seen his father only a few times since his dad was committed to a mental hospital years ago. His mother is a Christian, and in spite of all the trouble they have had, her son is also a Christian.

"This boy knew that I wasn't the 'nicest' girl around. He knew I needed God in my life. On our first date he told me that I needed to ask to be forgiven for my sins. That got to me right then. As he talked I realized that God was the someone I needed.

"I was truly changed that night. I am thankful to God that I found the one I love very much now, and through him found God. We plan to marry and raise our children in the best home that we can. And by the grace of God, we will.

"What does this have to do with today's 'pleasure seekers'? Lots. If we hate the world our parents are leaving for us, we certainly don't want to leave it the same or worse for our kids, do we? Then it is our job to do our best with what we've got. And nothing can be best without God.

"I close now, praying that my words will speak to others who are unconsciously searching for that 'special something.'"

Are young people searching for something higher and greater

*than they realize? What would have happened if the Christian
boy this girl met had felt it would be dangerous to have anything
to do with her? Are there risks in having dates or close contacts
with someone who lives as this teen-age girl did? Are there
some risks we should take for God?*

*Could you say something to a spiritually restless person as
helpful as the Christian boy did? How does a person learn to
witness like that?*

*If you had twenty-four hours to do whatever you wanted,
what would you do? What does the way a person enjoys himself
(or herself) say about his character?*

YOUNG PEOPLE AND THE FUTURE

What do young people think about the world they are growing up in? Certainly not all of them think alike, but Dr.
Margaret Mead, the world-famous American anthropologist,
points out in her book *Culture and Commitment: A Study of
the Generation Gap* that all of them are alike in one thing:
They have all been born into a world that is completely different from any that previously existed. For one thing, only
within this generation has it become possible for one person
or group to destroy all life on earth. For another, only within
this generation has man so fouled his environment that he is
unwittingly destroying many living things and quite possibly
himself. And only within this generation has it become possible
for the world to be one, for all mankind to achieve instant
communication and a "global village." Never before were
men able to explore outer space, or to see close-up the horrors
of war, even though it may be fought on the other side of
the globe.

The way many young people feel is voiced by a fifteen-year-
old Texas boy named Shannon Dickson[1]:

[1] Doubleday & Company, Inc. Copyright © 1970 by Margaret Mead. Used
by permission.

"There is a mass confusion in the minds of my generation in trying to find a solution for ourselves and the world around us.

"We see the world as a huge rumble as it swiftly goes by with wars, poverty, prejudice, and the lack of understanding among people and nations.

"Then we stop and think: There must be a better way and we have to find it.

"We see the huge rat race of arguing people trying to beat their fellow man out. All of this builds up, causing unrest between nations and in the home. My generation is being used almost like a machine. We are to learn set standards, strive for better education so we can follow in our elders' footsteps. But why? If we are to be a generation of repetition, the situation will be worse. But how shall we change? We need a great deal of love for everyone, we need a universal understanding among people, we need to think of ourselves and to express our feelings, but that is not all. I have yet to discover what else we need, nor have I practiced these things as fully as I should. Because when I try I am sneered at by my elders and those who do not hear, or look at it with a closed mind. Computers take the place of minds; electronics are taking over, only confusing things more.

"I admit we should follow some basic rules, but first you should look at who is making the rules.

"Sometimes I walk down a deserted beach listening to the waves and birds and I hear them forever calling and forever crying and sometimes we feel that way but everyone goes on with his own little routines, afraid to stop and listen for fear of cracking their nutshell.

"The answer is out there somewhere. We need to search for it."

Do you agree that "there must be a better way" than prejudice, worldwide hunger, and global murder through war? Does the world need a change? Isn't change what Christianity is supposed to be all about? But—"how shall we change?" How would you answer this boy's question? Is quoting a religious formula enough? Are there young people at whom we, too, sneer or look down at patronizingly? Is there an answer to questions that a youth like this one is asking? Is the answer "out there somewhere"? How are we—or they—going to find it?

YOUNG PEOPLE AND THE FUTURE: The Strange New World Beginning Now

The twentieth century began with tremendous hope. Science had produced a fantastic world of horseless carriages and steam-powered caravans, of machines that could do the work of many men, of knowledge that led back to the beginning of the world, of eyes that reached to strange secrets in space. Wise men had mastered the arts of government, they believed, and turned to the accomplishing of a world without war. Monarchies and superstitions were definitely on the decline, democracies and rationality assuredly on the rise. America had survived the threat of civil-war division and was consolidating its island territories.

The question today is whether we will make it to the year 2000. At the turn of 1970, a European biologist has said that life on earth will probably end within thirty-five to one hundred years. Dr. Paul Ehrlich has said that water pollution, air pollution and overpopulation will produce "the greatest cataclysm in the history of man," perhaps before 1980. Nobel Prize winner and Harvard biology professor George Wald says that we are headed for "total chaos"—"probably within the next ten years."

Dr. Max Blumer, a senior scientist at the famous Woods Hole Oceanographic Institution, who has been making a study of oil pollution in the ocean, has found that it is killing all kinds of marine life, that it is polluting the whole ocean, and that it is irreversible. After enough time, rivers and lakes can renew themselves, but the ocean cannot. And ocean life is also being killed by nitrates and phosphates from fertilizers, from

244

radioactive wastes, and from the poisons the military has been creating in the name of defense.

Why worry about the ocean? Because this is the source of most of the oxygen we breathe. In the past, the trees and the ocean could replace the oxygen we used up, but we are cutting down our trees, destroying the jungles of Southeast Asia, and our pollutants are killing the tiny ocean creatures that create new oxygen. So we may soon run out of breathable air.

We are in a strange new world that will destroy the life that is destroying it unless we can change our ways radically and speedily. In her book *Culture and Commitment,* anthropologist Margaret Mead says that all of us who were born before World War II are immigrants in this new age as surely as our forefathers were immigrants in North America, and that just as immigrants from the Old World found their old ways of little value here but had to learn from their children, so we will have to learn from our children how to live in the world of the atom and imminent destruction.

"The young generation, however," writes Dr. Mead, "the articulate young rebels all around the world who are lashing out against the controls to which they are subjected, are like the first generation born into a new country. They are at home in this time. . . . When they are given the facts, they can understand immediately that continued pollution of the air and water and soil will soon make the planet uninhabitable and that it will be impossible to feed an indefinitely expanding world population. . . . they recognize that invidious distinction based on race and caste are anachronisms. They insist on the vital necessity of some form of world order."

When most of us think of young people, we think in terms of teaching them something. Is it possible we could learn some important things from them? Two thousand years ago some of the wisest religious leaders of their time could have learned much from a twelve-year-old boy sitting in their midst, in Jerusalem. Can we learn from the youth in our midst? How?

Many educational, government, and religious groups are adding young people to the boards and committees that make the decisions and set the policies. Is this a wise move? How can young people help us? What can we do to make this possible?

See also POLLUTION AND US, STEWARDSHIP.

YOUNG PEOPLE AND LONG HAIR: Nightmare or Opportunity?

An educational journal[1] published a picture of a young man who might be a teacher's nightmare: headband over shoulder-length hair, a mustache and beard, a sort of bandanna around the neck of his open-throat shirt. "This young man," the publication said editorially, "is an apparition from a school administrator's darkest dream. He is an affront to our most cherished values: short hair, white shirts, moderate sideburns. He violates our image as the right sort of youth."

The hippie-looking youth, however, the journal went on, may be more of an opportunity to educators than the crewcut young man who has become a dropout, or the well-dressed young executive whose highest goal is paying for his second car. "These young men are more familiar and therefore more 'acceptable' —yet it is they, and not our hippie, who tend to ignore the problems of society. . . . [We may seek to avoid him because he] asks us embarrassing questions, challenges our ability to cope with some very unpleasant facts, even casts doubts on our achievements. . . . Our refusal to talk has turned discussion into confrontation. Any further refusal could turn confrontation into revolution. The young man with the long hair is still, essentially, playing on our side. Isn't it time for us to see who our friends are?"

Appearances have some importance, but are they as important as what a person thinks and desires? Is long hair an unpardonable sin? If we lived in a town below a dam that was about to break, would we be grateful to the person who brought us news of the danger? Wouldn't it be easier to ignore the

[1] *Education,* published by the New York State Education Department.

warning and hope nothing would happen? Prophets in unlikely garb sometimes bothered the ancient Hebrews so much that they were lynched—even though their warnings happened to be accurate.

Mrs. Billy Graham, interviewed in the December, 1969, *Woman's Day*, said: "I've learned that the students with beards are usually more interesting. I may not agree with them, but I'm always stimulated. They're original and they have the courage to be different."

Are there young people you "write off" because of their appearance? How would Jesus react to them? What would happen if you tried to become their friend?

YOUNG PEOPLE AND THEIR MANIFESTOES

With all the ultimatums, take-overs, demonstrations and manifestoes of young people today, it is easy to get the impression that protesting youth are mentally sick or manipulated by subversive forces. Quite a different impression emerges as one actually listens to what many of our youth are asking or saying, and as one discovers what they are concerned about. At the Pennsylvania Convention of the American Baptists in Scranton in 1969, the Young Churchmen of that denomination presented "A Modest Manifesto" which said in part:

"Change is the word that describes our age . . . the Spirit blows where it will and not always as we expect or direct it.

"Jesus was one who worshiped God in his accustomed place, but most of his ministry was where the people were crushed, hurting, broken. The world is broken with hate and war, our nation is prostituted by militarism and materialism and sick with both blatant and subtle racism. So virulent are these ills that even the church is infected.

"We call on the Pennsylvania Baptist Convention, in the light of the day in which we live, with both its problems and its promise, to be willing to re-evaluate all its priorities. . . .

247

We believe staff portfolios need to be re-evaluated with an eye to freeing staff to help train local congregations (which are often sadly locked into a static situation) to make a difference where they live, because the Bible calls for more action than most of us are willing to credit it for. . . .

"How long will God tolerate an irresponsible use of his leaven which has been designed for his world? Christians today are sinners in the hands of an angry God because we have domesticated his gospel. . . .

"Young Churchmen are opting for life—exciting, energizing, Spirit-guided, not only for ourselves, but for the whole church and the whole world, beginning as it always must, with us and our relationship with Christ."

Aren't the Young Churchmen's questions worth thinking about, praying about, and doing something about—in any church group? Is it possible that the church today is not being stirred so much by subversives or trouble-makers or unbelievers as by God Himself? He said to Jeremiah (21:27), "I will overturn, overturn, overturn . . . until he come whose right it is; and I will give it him." Isn't it exciting and encouraging that there are many young people who have not left the church but who are working in it, trying to help it find its place in this crucial hour in the redemption of mankind?

YOUNG PEOPLE AND RULES

One of the changes in American life during the 1960s was the almost complete disappearance of rules and regulations from college dormitories. Boys and girls are free to remain in one another's rooms as long as they wish on many campuses, and coed dorms are replacing those that were once segregated by sex.

In many cases, notes Paul Woodring, the new nonregulation interferes with learning. "Some girls report that the freedom to entertain boys in their rooms makes it extremely difficult to terminate a date without offending the boy, and consequently difficult to get enough sleep. Freshmen of both sexes find it difficult to avoid being drawn into activities, such as the use of illegal drugs, that they would prefer to avoid. The strain placed upon the student who wants to live within the law and the mores is great, particularly if he is eager to be popular with his peers."[1]

Is it fair to young people to take away the rules that used to guide and help many of them? If they are expected to make their own decisions, have we adults provided them with the necessary information and insights? Would not even mature adults be placed under strain in a modern college? Psychiatrists say that even though they would disclaim this, most young people want and need the security of definite rules. Do you agree? If not, what is the answer?

YOUNG PEOPLE AND SEX: Is There a Sex Revolution?

In an interview with L. I. Stell, Dr. Benjamin Spock expressed the belief that there is no "sexual revolution" today.[2] In fact, he took issue strongly with those young people who say sex "is merely a hope and instinct that is meant to be enjoyed as long as no one is hurt." He continued:

"This incredible view—life-style—can lead to pain and despair. It mechanizes sex. . . . It is crazy to think that you can get over the guiltiness of sex or shame about sex. These have different, specific, moral connotations in different societies, but basically it's the feeling that sex belongs to your parents, and the only legitimate way you can get to it is to become a parent yourself. The Catholic Church, in this sense, is entirely right. It is crazy and immoral to teach sexuality without teaching the spiritual aspects of sexuality; yet it is hard to

[1] *The Saturday Review,* December 20, 1969, p. 63.
[2] *Tempo,* December 1, 1969.

say these things without giving the young people the idea that you're trying to deny them sexual pleasure . . . never kid yourself that you are going to turn sex into something that's simple and pleasurable like eating. . . . Know that it's an incredibly complicated system out of which the whole of civilization has grown."

There may be no sexual revolution, but modern civilization makes sex more available and less restricted than ever before. Does this spell a new sex morality? Would we do well to listen to Dr. Spock and to all the cultures that have treated sex as somehow sacred, holy, and restricted? Does such a view restrict young people's freedom, or is it simply common sense?

One meaning of "morality" limits it to sexual ethics. Should it be so restricted? What is morality? Is it true, as some say today, that morality has nothing to do with what two adults choose to do between themselves? On the other hand, is personal morality more important than public or national or business or civic morality?

YOUNG PEOPLE AND WAR: Vietnam

The young people of America have been more active, perhaps, than their elders, both for and against this country's involvement in the war in Vietnam. One of the most effective statements some of us have seen on the subject was written by a twelve-year-old girl in Florida named Barbara Ellen Beidler. Barbara's poem caused a national flap; after the Presbyterian magazine *Venture* printed it early in 1967, the United States Defense Department canceled its 13,000 subscriptions to that periodical. Then, after this brought publicity throughout the world, the Department reinstated the subscriptions.

Here is the poem, reprinted from *Venture*.[1]

[1] Reprinted from *Venture*, copyright © 1967 The Geneva Press. Used by permission of the publisher and the author.

Afterthoughts on Napalm Drop on Jungle Villages Near Haiphong

By Barbara Ellen Beidler

All was still.
The sun rose through silver pine boughs
Over sleeping green-straw huts,
Over cool rice ponds,
Through the emerald jungles,
Into the sky.
The men rose and went out to the fields
and ponds.
The women set pots on fire, boiling
rice and jungle berries, and some
with baskets went for fish.
The children played in the streams and
danced through the weeds.
Then there was the flash—silver and
gold
Silver and gold,
Silver birds flying,
Golden water raining.
The rice ponds blazed with new water.
The jungles burst into gold and sent
up little birds of fire.
Little animals with fur of flame.
Then the children flamed.
Running—their clothes flying like fiery
kites.
Screaming—their screams dying as
their faces seared.
The women's baskets burned on their
heads.
The men's boats blazed on the rice
waters.
Then the rains came.
A rag, fire black, fluttered.

A curl of smoke rose from a lone rice
    stem.
The forest lay singed, seared.
A hut crumbled.
And all was still.
Listen, Americans,
Listen clear and long.
The children are screaming
In the jungles of Haiphong.

*What do these lines say to you? How do you explain to
a child why the most powerful nation in the world feels it
has to burn children alive in one of the weakest, hungriest
countries? Is this a statement against one war, or against all
wars? What should our attitude be toward those young people
whose conscience forbids them to take part in a particular war?
In this age, is war an acceptable way of settling national
disputes? Does war ever settle anything?*

For reference: Matthew 5:9; Titus 3:9; Matthew 26:52;
Proverbs 15:16; Ecclesiastes 10:4; Isaiah 32:17; I Thessalonians 5:13; James 4:1-4.

APPENDIX

Denominational

African Methodist Episcopal Church, 414 8th Avenue South, Nashville, Tennessee 37203.

African Methodist Episcopal Zion Church, Box 508, Charlotte, North Carolina 28201.

American Baptist Association, 214 East Broad Street, Texarkana, Arkansas 75501.

American Baptist Convention, Valley Forge, Pennsylvania 19481.

American Lutheran Church, 442 South 5th Street, Minneapolis, Minnesota 55415.

Assemblies of God, 1445 Boonville Avenue, Springfield, Missouri 65802.

Christian Churches (Disciples of Christ), Christian Board of Publication, Beaumont and Pine Boulevard, St. Louis, Missouri 63166.

Christian Methodist Episcopal Church, 6524 16th Street Northwest, Washington, D.C. 20012.

Christian and Missionary Alliance, Nyack, New York 10960.

Christian Reformed Church, 2850 Kalamazoo Avenue Southeast, Grand Rapids, Michigan 49508.

Church of the Brethren, 1451 Dundee Avenue, Elgin, Illinois 60120.

Church of God (Anderson, Indiana), Box 2499, Anderson, Indiana 46011.

Church of God (Cleveland, Tennessee), Keith Street at 25th, Cleveland, Tennessee 37311.

Church of the Nazarene, 6401 The Paseo, Kansas City, Missouri 64131.

Conservative Baptist Association of America, Box 66, Wheaton, Illinois 60187.

Episcopal Church, 815 Second Avenue, New York, New York 10017.

Evangelical Covenant Church of America, 5101 North Francisco Avenue, Chicago, Illinois 60625.

Evangelical Free Church of America, 1515 East 66th Street, Minneapolis, Minnesota 55423.

Free Methodist Church of North America, Winona Lake, Indiana 46590.

Free Will Baptists, 1134 Murfreesboro Road, Nashville, Tennessee 37217.

Friends United Meeting, 101 Quaker Hill Drive, Richmond, Indiana 47374.

General Association of Regular Baptist Churches, 1500 Oakton Boulevard, Des Plaines, Illinois 60018.

Lutheran Church—Missouri Synod, 3558 South Jefferson Avenue, St. Louis, Missouri 63118.

Mennonite Church, Scottdale, Pennsylvania 15683.

National Baptist Convention of America, 319 21st Street, Nashville, Tennessee 37206.

National Baptist Convention, U.S.A., Inc., 330 Charlotte Avenue, Nashville, Tennessee 37201.

North American Baptist Association, 716 Main Street, Little Rock, Arkansas 72201.

Pentecostal Church of God of America, Inc., 312 Joplin Avenue, Joplin, Missouri 64801.

Presbyterian Church in the U.S., Box 1176, Richmond, Virginia 23209.

Progressive National Baptist Convention, Inc., 470 Wooster Avenue, Akron, Ohio 44307.

Reformed Church in America, 475 Riverside Drive, New York, New York 10027.

Religious Society of Friends (General Conference), 1520 Race Street, Philadelphia, Pennsylvania 19102.

Salvation Army, 120 West 14th Street, New York, New York 10011.

Seventh-day Adventists, 6840 Eastern Avenue N.W., Washington, D.C. 20012.

Southern Baptist Convention, 127 9th Avenue N., Nashville, Tennessee 37203.

United Church of Christ, 1505 Race Street, Philadelphia, Pennsylvania 19102.

United Methodist Church, 1001 Nineteenth Avenue S., Nashville, Tennessee 37202.

United Pentecostal Church, Inc., 3645 South Grand Boulevard, St. Louis, Missouri 63118.

United Presbyterian Church in the U.S.A., Witherspoon Building, Philadelphia, Pennsylvania 19107.

Wesleyan Methodist Church of America, Box 2000, Marion, Indiana 46952.

Interdenominational

David C. Cook Publishing Company, Elgin, Illinois 60120.

Gospel Light Publications, Glendale, California 91209.

Scripture Press, 1825 College Avenue, Wheaton, Illinois 60187.

Standard Publishing, 8121 Hamilton Avenue, Cincinnati, Ohio 45231.

Union Gospel Press, 2030 Brook Park, Cleveland, Ohio 44109.

RELIGIOUS PERIODICALS

The news media and what used to be called "the secular world" are full of marvelous illustrations for anyone trying to communicate religious truth. In the religious world, the following publications strike me as particularly useful for this purpose. Each paper or magazine has its own special values.

America, 106 West 56th Street, New York, New York 10019.

American Baptist, Valley Forge, Pennsylvania 19481.

Catholic Digest, 2959 North Hamline Avenue, St. Paul, Minnesota 55113.

The Christian Century, 407 South Dearborn Street, Chicago, Illinois 60605.

Christian Herald, 27 East 39th Street, New York, New York 10016.

Christianity and Crisis, 537 West 121st Street, New York, New York 10027.

Christianity Today, 1014 Washington Building, Washington, D.C. 20005.

Commonweal, 232 Madison Avenue, New York, New York 10016.

The Episcopalian, 1930 Chestnut Street, Philadelphia, Pennsylvania 19103.

Eternity, 1716 Spruce Street, Philadelphia, Pennsylvania 19103.

Faith at Work, Box 1790, Waco, Texas 76703.

Gospel Herald, Scottdale, Pennsylvania 15683.

Guideposts, Carmel, New York 10512.

International Journal of Religious Education, 475 Riverside Drive, New York, New York 10027.

The Lutheran, 2900 Queen Lane, Philadelphia, Pennsylvania 19129.

National Catholic Reporter, Box 281, Kansas City, Missouri 64141.

Our Sunday Visitor, Noll Plaza, Huntington, Indiana 46750.

Presbyterian Life, Witherspoon Building, Philadelphia, Pennsylvania 19107.

Presbyterian Outlook, 512 East Main Street, Richmond, Virginia 23219.

The Sign, Monastery Place, Union City, New Jersey 07087.

Tempo, Box 81, Madison Square Station, New York, New York 10010.

Together, Box 423, Park Ridge, Illinois 60068.

United Church Herald, 297 Park Avenue South, New York, New York 10010.

The United Church Observer, 85 St. Clair Avenue East, Toronto 290, Ontario, Canada.

Western Catholic Reporter, 11645 Jasper Avenue, Edmonton 11, Alberta, Canada.

INDEX

Micah, 74
Migrant workers, 45, 48
Military defense, 21, 23, 82–83, 124–25, 158–60
Military destruction, 48, 149
Military-industrial complex, 158
Military weapons, 36
Ministers
  definition, 59–60
  support of, 57–59
Ministry, 92
Minorities, 136
Missions, 50
Mistakes, 142–43
Money, 143–45
Monod, Jacques, 146
Moods, low, 176
Moon exploration, 27, 195
Morality, 60, 63–64, 92, 144–47, 214–17
Moral standards, 122, 144–45
Moses, 107, 149

Nader, Ralph, 145, 194
Nature, 31, 207–8
Nazism, 72, 80–81, 84, 231
Neanderthal man, 66
New Catholicism, 69
Nuclear destruction, 149
Nudity, 37

Obedience, 71
Open mind, 151–52
Openness, 152–54, 235
Overpopulation, 244

Paine, Thomas, 20
Past, the, 154
Paton, Alan, 62, 100, 146, 176, 210
Patriotism, 18, 154–57, 163
Paul (Apostle), 49, 58, 79, 147, 158
Peace, 23, 82–83, 156–60, 212–13, 218–19

Peace symbol, 158
Pearl Harbor, 20, 27
Personal encounter, 70
Personal experience, 185
Personal responsibility, 185
Pesticides, 131, 168
Plato, 108
Pleasure, 162–63
Politics, 48
Pollution, 48, 163–64, 168, 244
Poor, the, 48, 75–76, 144, 164–69, 229–30
  diseases of, 75
  health of, 167–69
Population explosion, 244
Potok, Chaim, 108
Power, 21
Prayer, 84, 232–33
  answers to, 169–73
  freedom in, 178
  nature of, 173–75
  for peace, 156–57
  rules of, 169–72
Priorities, 21
Prisons, 73–75, 178–79
Private property, 64–66
Problem solving, 179
Propaganda and Scripture, 196
Prophetic insight, 56
Prophetic role, 29
Protests, 48, 180
Psalms, 175–78
Puerto Ricans, 75
Punishment, 178–79
  legal, 73
Puritans, 229

Race relationships, 32–34, 36, 37, 57, 125, 181–82, 220, 239–40
Reality, ultimate, 217–18
Reality of the invisible, 31
Reality therapy, 31
Reason, failure of, 189